CONTENTS

DRIBBLES OF CHAMPIONS

Selected tales from the Cleveland Cavaliers'
remarkable run to the title

SAM AMICO

Copyright © 2016 Sam Amico All rights reserved.

Printed in the United States of America. Except as permitted under the United States Copyright Act of 1976, no part of this publication may be reproduced or distributed in any form or by any means, or stored in a database or retrieval system, without the prior written permission of the author.

ISBN-13: 978-1537763552
ISBN-10: 1537763555

For Katie, Brady, James and Baby. We make quite a starting five.

ACKNOWLEDGMENTS

No project or coverage of a professional sports organization can exist without the assistance of the media relations staff, so thanks to Tad Carper and all who serve that role for the Cavaliers. Also thanks to members of the FOX Sports Ohio team who offer helpful suggestions during the season: Brent Valenti, Gene Winters, Joe Ranyak, Campy Russell, Bruce Drennan, Fred McLeod, Austin Carr, Dan Larson and lifelong friend Jeff Phelps.

INTRODUCTION

It wasn't until Warriors guard and back-to-back MVP Steph Curry missed his final 3-pointer that most fans believed the Cavaliers would actually win the NBA championship.

Curry's errant shot came with about five seconds left in Game 7, and the Cavs were up by four points. So even if his shot it went in, the Cavs still would have led by a point, with the ball, and maybe two seconds left.

Yet most fans probably kept thinking, "What next?" Or worse, "Wonder how we're gonna blow it this time?"

That's just the way Cleveland fans always thought, and you couldn't blame them.

The Drive. The Fumble. Red Right 88. The Shot. Jose Mesa in 1997.

Cleveland sports fans had seen it all, and none of it was good.

At least, not since 1964, when pro football's Browns won what had been the city's last major sports title.

After that, it was 52 years of disappointing finishes and sometimes, utter heartbreak. ESPN even made a documentary about it called *Believeland*.

It chronicled Cleveland's sports failures, the many times the Browns, Cavs and Indians came oh so close ... and failed.

But Cleveland sports fans didn't need a documentary. The city lived through it, year after year, tear after tear. Maybe ESPN just figured the rest of the world needed to know what sports distress truly felt like it.

After all, when it came to anguish, Cleveland was the undisputed champ.

But somehow, LeBron James, Kyrie Irving and the rest of the 2015-16 Cavaliers changed all that. They ended the nightmare. And if not a nightmare, then a continuous kick to the gut.

For Cleveland, it couldn't have come against a better basketball opponent. The Warriors became to the Cavs almost what the Steelers were to the Browns.

The Warriors defeated a Cavs team missing Irving and Kevin Love in the previous year's finals. Then the Warriors swept the Cavs in the 2015-16 regular season -- first on Christmas Day, then by 32 points on the Cavs' home floor.

That's right. Thirty-two points. In Cleveland.

The Cavs returned to the finals, onlyto fall flat at first. The Warriors raced and trash-talked their way to a 3-1 series lead in the rematch.

Cleveland fans had to be thinking, "There's always next year. Maybe." Again.

The Warriors ran their mouths, flexed after made baskets and danced on the sidelines, Curry and Draymond Green leading their obnoxious charge.

All along the way, they garnered what seemed like clear favoritism from

1

the jump-on-the-bandwagon national media.

At least, it must have felt like favoritism to Cleveland fans. Not only did Cleveland teams not win championships, but the entire world was against them. It really did often seem that way.

And then the Warriors blew it. Man, did they ever blow it. They blew it like no other team in NBA history.

More accurately, LeBron James and the Cavs just took it. They refused to go down again. They shut up everyone who said all season that "they can't play like that and beat the Warriors."

They didn't just bring a championship to Cleveland for the first time in 52 years. In the final three games, they dominated an opponent that finished 73-9, the best record in regular-season history. The Warriors appeared invincible.

But they weren't as invincible as Cleveland. Not when it mattered most.

When it mattered most, this time, it was Cleveland that rose to the occasion. The Cavaliers. Cleveland. Champions.

What follows is my own journey covering the team, with selected columns and features from 2015-16 to help fans relive the drama, and amazing ending, of a season they will remember forever.

The goal of this book isn't to find a spot on the New York Times' bestseller list. It never will. Rather, it's meant as keepsake for Cleveland sports fans who so badly deserve it.

You've come a long way, baby.

1 ASPIRATIONS

OCTOBER 23

Blatt tries to calm title hype

David Blatt is aware general managers across the NBA have picked the Cavaliers as the NBA's next champion. It's safe to say he's not entirely caught up in all of that, either.

"What do GMs know?" Blatt asked.

The second-year Cavs coach was just having a little fun. But his point was clear: There are still games to be played, and lots of them.

And as we saw with last year's LeBron James-led team, things like needing time to adapt and injuries to key players at the worst possible time can alter your expectations quickly and considerably.

So predictions about what might happen in June?

Hey, Blatt doesn't want to hear it.

"We're not even talking about that right now," he said. "We're talking about how we can get everybody on the same page, get all our players back, work hard and try to make day-to-day progress."

Blatt and James propelled the Cavs to the Finals in their first season together. Nearly everything was new at this time last year — as Blatt was a first-time NBA coach, James was returning to the franchise that drafted him after four years with the Heat, and Kevin Love was playing in Cleveland for the first time after a successful career with the Timberwolves.

That was just the beginning. Younger holdovers Kyrie Irving, Tristan Thompson and Dion Waiters were learning how to win after several seasons of missing the playoffs.

Later, Waiters was traded and J.R. Smith, Iman Shumpert and Timofey Movgov were brought in.

Not long after that, things really began to click.

Not long after that, the playoffs came — and Love went down in the first round with a shoulder injury, followed by Irving in the Finals with a knee issue.

James tried with all his might to carry the Cavs to their first title, but despite an historic individual performance, the Cavs succumbed to the Warriors in six difficult games.

PAINS REMAIN

Today, some of those injury predicaments linger.

Love is slowly working his way back after about five months off. Irving remains out and is likely to miss the first four weeks of the season, possibly more. Shumpert (wrist surgery) could be out until February. Movgov indicated his knee is bothering him.

And no less than James just recently took an anti-inflammatory injection to his sometimes-achy lower back.

"We're being very conscientious and cautious with him," Blatt said of James. "He's fine and he's going to be fine. But we're going slowly and carefully with him."

On the bright side, James and Love are expected to play in Tuesday's season opener at the Bulls.

The Cavs have also welcomed back Tristan Thompson (holdout) and Anderson Varejao (Achilles), and have added key veterans such as Mo Williams and Richard Jefferson, and 30-year old Russian rookie Sasha Kaun.

No matter, while the survey of NBA GMs and their projection of very good things are nice, Blatt knows tons of stuff can happen between now and when the season matters most.

"That's very far down the line," Blatt said. "What we're really concerned with is just becoming a good team right now."

Makes sense. After all, what do GMs know, anyway?

OCTOBER 27

Finally, will this be the Cavaliers' year?

LeBron James knows it can happen. Despite what David Blatt says, Blatt knows it can, too. And you can be sure Kyrie Irving and Kevin Love believe.

The question in play is if the Cavaliers can win the first championship in franchise history. The answer, to a man, is always the same.

"Yes, of course," says James.

These are hardly earth-shattering proclamations booming from the Cavs' practice facility.

Of course the Cavs believe they can win it all. They came oh-so-close last season. They won the East despite a 19-20 start, lots of allegations and reported (some true but mostly otherwise) drama.

They managed to split the first two games of the Finals, on the road, without Irving and Love and a whole lot of Matthew Dellavedova on Steph Curry.

But eventually, the Cavs just ran out of gas. The Warriors were just too talented, too smart, too sharp. The Cavs, despite an otherworldly performance from James, were just too undermanned.

They're starting the season in a similar spot Tuesday at Chicago.

Irving remains out following knee surgery in June. Iman Shumpert (wrist) is missing with a surgical repair of his own. Love is recovering from a shoulder injury and James is dealing with a lower back that can sometimes be a pain.

But the vibe entering the season?

Well, now. That's nothing like it was last season.

Blatt is no longer new to the NBA. You can just hear a relaxed and quiet confidence when he speaks. He clearly has a firm grasp of how to deal with a team that has a super-duper star, a couple of other stars, and warrants lots of attention — including some of the unwanted kind.

James and the others know what to expect from Blatt and his coaching staff, too.

Read: This is no longer the first year with this program. This is a team that has experienced the ups and downs of an NBA season, a year of fame, of consistently being under a microscope.

The Cavs' every move is overanalyzed and often criticized. And now they're used to it. And now they don't care. And now there are no more talks of contracts and players wanting to leave — as Love, Tristan Thompson and LeBron himself have all returned.

They're all clearly here for the long term. They're all free of distractions.

This isn't to say things will go perfectly. This isn't to say the Cavs won't be criticized or overanalyzed again. This isn't to say basketball reporters will conduct themselves like princes and princesses or stick to reporting about basketball.

But as James often says, there's nothing he hasn't seen. There's little this version of the Cavs have not seen, too.

ANOTHER JOURNEY

There will be obstacles.

The Bulls will be refreshed under relaxed and player-friendly new coach Fred Hoiberg. The Hawks are very good and tired of hearing they are not. The Heat are hoping for one last chance. No less than Dwyane Wade told James that the Heat are "coming for him."

And that's just the East.

The Warriors were no fluke, and if there's anything that can offer a champion motivation, it's everyone suggesting they may not have been for real.

The Spurs, the Rockets, the Clippers, the Grizzlies, the Thunder — fortunately for the Cavs, those West powers must fight amongst themselves.

But it may not matter.

James, Love and Irving may all be healthy when it means the most. Same goes for Shumpert and perhaps Anderson Varejao.

Other key pieces such as Timofey Mozgov, J.R. Smith, Mo Williams, Richard Jefferson and Thompson may again fit in well.

And Blatt may prove to be the coach that can bring it all together.

The Cavaliers came close last season. Oh so close. Can they do it again? Can they take it another step?

It won't be easy, but with good health, it could very well be easier.

OCTOBER 28

Not a win, but Cavs show promise of champion

Most everyone who follows the NBA suspects this will be the Cavaliers' year.

And even in season-opening defeat, the Cavs gave a few examples why.

Yes, the Cavs dropped a 97-95 road decision to the Bulls. Yes, they had a chance at the end -- only to have their last gasp fall flat. And yes, they displayed several areas in which there's room to improve.

But hey, as far as season openers go, it sure beats last season.

Last season, the Cavs opened at home to tons of buzz. LeBron James was back. Kevin Love was in town. Kyrie Irving was still a key member of the team. And David Blatt was making his NBA coaching debut.

And the Cavs went kaput -- and to the lowly New York Knicks to boot.

This time, hype is an afterthought. Everyone understands the Cavs' potential, assuming they get (and stay) relatively healthy.

Much like the end of last season, the Cavs are without Irving, who's still recovering from knee surgery in June. They're also minus Iman Shumpert (wrist surgery), their starting shooting guard in the Finals.

But they were right there, on the road, against a very good team -- with an opportunity to tie or win at the end.

"That's all you can ask," James told reporters in Chicago.

And there was plenty of good news to come out of it.

James scored 25 points and pulled down 10 rebounds. Love went for 18 and eight, respectively. That included two big 3-pointers near the end to give the Cavs their fighting chance.

And old friend/newcomer Mo Williams filled in for Irving at point guard to the tune of 19 points and seven assists.

But those are just numbers from one night. One night that, aside from perhaps President Barack Obama's presence, doesn't really mean a whole lot.

What's more telling is how the Cavs stuck with it, how they dug deep when everyone else in the building wanted them to fail, how you could tell that none of this was new to them.

Basically, they didn't know what to expect last season. They knew they'd be really good -- they just didn't really seem sure how to go about getting there.

Today, though, not much is new.

Blatt knows his players and his players know the coaching staff.

James knows Love, Love knows Tristan Thompson (12 rebounds), Thompson knows Timofey Mozgov, Mozgov knows J.R. Smith ... on and on it goes.

And these Cavs know winning. They know surviving. They know the regular season is one massive basketball marathon, and that what matters most is to play your best at the end.

That's not to say they were content with final result Tuesday. It's just that they understand what happens now isn't the end of the world, nor the beginning of something great -- regardless of whether things bounce their way.

It's just a time to improve, to show the rest of the league they're truly the force everyone says they are, and a team that isn't as concerned with finding its way as it is with letting that way come to it.

The Cavs lost a close game to a good team on the road on opening night. That's really all you need to know about the first game.

The rest, and the best, is likely yet to come.

OCTOBER 30

LeBron still finding his range

CLEVELAND — Random dribbles on the Cavaliers heading into their home opener vs. the Heat.

1. LeBron James still needs to get his shot in order. That's not intended to be a harsh criticism — as LeBron has been mostly fantastic through the first two games. He also tends to make 'em when they count. (See Game 4 of playoffs at Chicago.) But he struggled with his perimeter shot for large chunks of last season and it's been more of the same this year.

2. James continues to be the best in the league at driving to the basket and finishing at the rim. That explains why he's shooting 46 percent (16-of-35 combined) in the first two games. But he's just 1-of-8 on 3-pointers, and worse, a miserable 4-of-11 on free throws.

3. Again, this is basically nitpicking. When it comes to potentially winning a championship, we all know James is the guy who will lead the Cavs. But his jumper isn't what it used to be, and if he can re-discover it, things will be that much easier on his achy lower back.

4. One of James' basketball heroes is Julius "Dr. J" Erving. Interestingly, Erving started primarily as a slasher and forceful dunker. But he reinvented himself later in his career by becoming a strong outside shooter. It's a major reason why Erving was able to be an effective (if not excellent) player until the moment he retired at age 36. Hitting perimeter shots saves your body from the wear and tear that comes with driving to the basket.

5. Overall, LeBron is averaging 18.5 points, 8.5 rebounds and 5.0 assists. Hard to complain about any of that.

6. As for the lower back, James underwent an MRI around the time he took that anti-inflammatory injection. The MRI showed no structural damage. So good news there.

7. Perhaps that's why LeBron gave the following answer when asked how many regular-season games he expects to play this season: "82."

8. Following Tuesday's cakewalk in Memphis, James indicated he suspects Kevin Love will be an All-Star this season. Love is undoubtedly off to an all-pro start — and just generally playing like a guy who understands how to win.

9. Read: It's always a good sign when a star player such as James sets individual goals (either for himself or for teammates). It means they think the team is good enough to handle a new set of challenges. Getting Love to the All-Star Game is one.

10. I've been particularly impressed with Mo Williams and Richard Jefferson. They're a large upgrade over last season's older vets Mike Miller and Shawn Marion – which is likely bad news for the rest of the league.

11. Williams can be streaky, but he's always amazed me with his ball-handling during the few times I've seen him work on it at practice. He may not be as flashy as Kyrie Irving or some of the other standout point guards, but Williams puts in the work and can really handle the rock.

12. Speaking of newcomers, the Cavs love young guard Jared Cunningham's

athleticism and willingness to learn. That said, keep an eye on second-year man Joe Harris. It seems the Cavs are beginning to question his potential after some of Harris' uneven play in the preseason.

13. James and the Cavs didn't fare too well vs. the Heat last season, starting with that stinker in Miami on Christmas Day. It will be interesting to see how LeBron handles facing his friends and former running-mates this time. Dwyane Wade has certainly tried to up the intensity by telling reporters the Heat "are coming for" LeBron.

14. After holding out for all but a few days of practice, Tristan Thompson has been as active as ever on the boards. He is averaging 10.0 rebounds through two games.

15. For those wondering, LeBron never pressured the Cavs during the Thompson contract talks. James did tell Thompson to do what he had to do — as well as reassure Thompson that he's important and needed.

16. As Jason Lloyd of the Akron Beacon Journal pointed out, James called for a team meeting between the end of the preseason and start of the regular season. No one is exactly sure what was said, but it was clearly the act of a champion aiming to get his guys to believe in and rely on one another.

17. Finally, I've covered the Cavs on and off for about 20 years, and I have never once – and I mean not ever — seen them move the ball as consistently well as they have in these first two games. It's beautiful basketball and Coach David Blatt deserves credit. Let's hope it continues.

NOVEMBER 20

LeBron, Cavs get back to what wins

CLEVELAND — Random dribbles from the Cavaliers' 115-100 win over the visiting Milwaukee Bucks on Thursday.

1. In terms of toughness and ball movement, that was much more like it. In the NBA, it's amazing how much easier things can be at home.

2. But for the Cavs (9-3), this was more than just feeling comfortable in their own gym after two straight losses on the road. It was deciding to play a certain way and making it happen.

3. Both LeBron James and Coach David Blatt talked about the Cavs' need to be tougher — both physically and mentally. They did that right from the beginning Thursday, with several hard, albeit usually clean, fouls when the Bucks neared the basket.

4. LeBron on the win: "We answered the call. We got better in some areas we wanted to get better in tonight."

5. James finished with 27 points on a sizzling 9-of-13 shooting, while Kevin Love put together one of his finest games of the early season. Love finished with 22 points and 15 rebounds – including 17 and seven in the first half. The Cavs also outscored the Bucks by 15 points with Love on the floor. Fittingly, that was the final margin.

6. But what you'll mostly read about is how Matthew Dellavedova stepped in for the injured Mo Williams at point guard, and how Delly directed the offense with precision to finish with a career-high 13 assists.

7. Blatt on Dellavedova: "What I liked about Delly's game tonight was that he made simple plays and he made them at the right times. He played the game solidly and simply and helped his team win."

8. Also, we're sure to hear plenty about Anderson Varejao, who gave a fine showing off the bench in his first action in three games. Varejao sat the entire first half, and it looked like he was headed for another night glued to a chair. But then Timoefy Mozgov went down with a shoulder injury (more on that in a minute), and Varejao ripped off his warmup and entered the game in third quarter.

9. It worked out well, too. Varejao made all four of his shots for nine points, grabbed a couple of rebounds, and just generally played like his typical energetic self on defense. "Andy really gave us a lift," was how Blatt put it.

10. This hasn't been an easy season for Varejao — or frankly, Cavs fans. When he's healthy, they're used to seeing him out there for no less than 25 minutes a night. This year? Varejao is averaging five minutes, if he plays at all.

11. After the game, Varejao repeatedly admitted it's been a difficult adjustment, "especially when you feel like you can still (contribute)."

12. But there are a few things to consider here. For one, he's 33-years old and coming off two seasons worth of major injuries. Plus, when he went down last season (with a torn Achilles), the Cavs had yet to trade for Mozgov. That trade happened in mid-January. Now, with Mozgov, Love and Tristan Thompson in the frontcourt, the big-man minutes are scarce, and someone is inevitably going to suffer.

13. J.R. Smith gave another fine showing, and seems to have emerged from his early-season shooting funk. Smith went 7-of-12 for 18 points. That included making half his eight 3-pointers.

14. Quick J.R. moment: After the game, he stood at his locker and checked out the Warriors-Clippers game on a large screen television. A couple of reporters marveled over how the Clippers' lead approached 20 points. Smith seemed unimpressed. "The Warriors gotta lose some time," he said. Then he paused and turned toward his locker, before turning back around and smiling. "Of course, I'd prefer it be us who beats them, but that's just me."

15. The Warriors, by the way, came back to win that game.

16. The Cavs finished with a whopping 29 assists on 40 made shots. When they move the ball like that ... well, the results are always favorable.

17. LeBron on ball movement: "That is just how we need to play. No ifs, ands or buts. Being able to move the ball is a good ingredient for us being successful. We also had 17 turnovers, but I felt some of those turnovers were aggressive turnovers that you can live with."

18. Meanwhile, Bucks power forward/small forward/shooting guard/and occasional center Giannis Antetokounmpo gave another exhilarating performance, scoring a career-high 33 points on 12-of-15 shooting. He was also 8-of-8 on free throws. All this and the 6-foot-11 athletic wonder doesn't turn 22 until December.

19. Blatt on Antekokounmpo: "Those are some pretty imposing numbers. That's a guy who has a tremendous future in this league."

20. The Cavs were also better at the line, finishing 21-of-26. And 80 percent is a heck of a lot better than what we've seen most of the season. James finished 8-of-9. "It starts with me," he said. "We're a good free-throw shooting team. We just went through some rough stretches."

21. Thompson added 12 points and 11 boards off the bench, and James Jones added nine. Overall, the Cavs got 39 points from the reserves, compared to 12 for the Bucks.

22. Williams was a game-time call after experiencing some leg soreness following Tuesday's loss at Detroit. He will receive some more treatment and his status for Saturday's home game vs. Atlanta remains up in the air.

23. Mozgov suffered a right shoulder strain in the first half. He will undergo an MRI and the Cavs will take it from there. So yes, they beat the Bucks while down at least three starters (Mozgov, Williams and Kyrie Irving) — and even a fourth if you believe Iman Shumpert will start upon returning from his wrist injury.

24. The Cavs are now 2-3 against the Central Division, 7-0 vs. the rest of the league.

2 RISE & SHINING

NOVEMBER 22

Just like that, Cavs rocking East again

CLEVELAND — Five dribbles on the Cavaliers' rather easy (no surprise there) 109-97 win over the visiting Atlanta Hawks on Saturday.

1. There was a time, like last year during the regular season, that the Cavs didn't seem to match up well with the Hawks. Then again, until about mid-January, the Cavs didn't really match up with anyone. But I suspect they won't start 19-20 again — and with the way things are going, the Hawks don't look like they pose much of a threat.

2. This isn't intended to rip the Hawks. They're still a top-five team in the East … I think. Let's count them out: A. Cavs. B. Bulls? C. Heat? D. Hawks? E. Hmmm. Pacers? I imagine the Raptors and Wizards figure in that race somewhere, too. But again, with the way the Cavs are looking, everyone else in the East is fighting for second.

3. It's still awful early, but this is sort of what I figured would happen with the Cavs (10-3). LeBron James (19 points, 11 rebounds) and Kevin Love (25 and 11) would consistently dominate, the Cavs would win a lot – and then Kyrie Irving and Iman Shumpert would return. And it'll be yikes, yikes and double yikes for a lot of opponents, if not for everyone.

4. Speaking of Irving, excellent ESPN beat guy Dave McMenamin reported Irving played James in a one-dribble-only game of one-on-one Saturday. According to McMenamin's source, Irving "destroyed" LeBron in one of the games. The two Cavs stars played a best-of-five set, per the report. No matter how you spin it, this is good news for the Cavs. Irving's return to full health will only make a really good team even better, and likely even more inspired.

5. I don't like how James got frustrated and removed himself from the game in the third quarter, without giving his replacement time to check in. It resulted in a technical foul for the Cavs. I do, however, like how James took responsibility for it afterward — admitting he "blew a gasket" and that he apologized to his teammates and coaches. True leadership doesn't mean being perfect. It means holding yourself accountable and showing your

teammates how to be a winner. LeBron, clearly, has been doing that for some time.

6. I always lie in these things. I said five dribbles. I'm writing a few more than that.

7. Cavs coach David Blatt on LeBron subbing himself out: "He thought we were playing hockey."

8. See how much fun it can be when things are going well? See how silly it was to freak out when the Cavs lost a couple of games last week? And man, the folks who love to stir up drama in search of web hits and TV ratings are terribly bored. When it comes to this year's Cavs, you can't even fabricate a good controversy.

9. Tristan Thompson finished with nine points and 16 boards, starting in place of Timofey Mozgov (shoulder). Matthew Dellavedova scored 12 points, in place of Mo Williams (sore leg), who is in place of Irving (knee). In fact, the Cavs outscored the Hawks by 27 points with Delly on the floor. Also, J.R. Smith scored 15 points on 5-of-18 shooting. Yes, that's a lot of misses, but the Cavs don't mind. They need Smith to be aggressive and keep firing away.

NOVEMBER 24

Lots of Love lifting Cavs higher

CLEVELAND — Random dribbles on the Cavaliers' 117-103 hammer job of the visiting Orlando Magic on Monday.

1. LeBron James has said he wants Kevin Love to make the All-Star team this season, and by the looks of things lately, James will get his wish. Love has been outstanding, and Monday night was perhaps the best example of a season that's going very right.

2. Love scored a season-high 27 points — in the first half. He finished with 34 — his highest output since joining the Cavs before the start of last season. What I like most about Love is how he's receiving the ball near the low blocks, backing down defenders, and scoring at the basket.

3. That's a change from last season, when it seemed like Love settled for 3-pointers way too often. Not a huge deal — as Love is one of the rare power

forwards who can nail shots from the perimeter and still pull down gobs of rebounds. But he also possesses a strong inside game that the Cavs didn't see nearly enough last year.

4. I suspect part of that was because Love's back was bothering him for about half the year. The other part was likely because the Cavs were truly a first-year program. LeBron returned to Cleveland, David Blatt debuted in the NBA, and Love and others were constantly trying to adjust to their new situation.

5. That said, Love still averaged 16.4 points and 9.7 rebounds. A lot of teams would kill to get those numbers from their so-called third option.

6. Through 13 games this year, those averages have increased to 18.3 points and 12.0 rebounds. Love is shooting 43 percent from the floor, 33 percent on threes, and a career-high 88 percent on free throws.

7. Yes, his field-goal percentage could afford to increase. But it's OK that Love has become a "volume shooter" of sorts. The Cavs need him to be aggressive and look to score.

8. Love on the night: "I found a good rhythm. I felt like I was posting up and my shot has felt great. It just hasn't quite dropped like it was tonight, at least (not) from the perimeter. Those guys were finding me, we were getting out on the break and getting easy looks. We've done a really good job these last few games, every single one of us, of going from a good shot to a great."

9. Moving on, J.R. Smith also seems to be rediscovering himself lately. He scored 26 on 10-of-16 shooting vs. the Magic, burying six of his 10 threes. Smith has scored at least 15 points in each of the previous four games. And if you exclude the 5-of-18 night vs. Atlanta, he's shooting a sizzling 61 percent in that span.

10. This is all good. Like Love, the Cavs need Smith to keep firing away. He can be streaky, but when he's on, it's usually a back-breaker to opponents.

11. Another cool thing about Monday: The Cavs starters crushed the Magic starters by a 99-44 count. What makes it even more impressive is some of these guys aren't actually Cavs starters. Instead, Matthew Dellavedova (15 points), Tristan Thompson (nine with 14 rebounds), and maybe even Smith will come off the bench when everyone is healthy.

12. Despite all that, LeBron will again warrant most of headlines for joining Oscar Robertson as the lone two players in league history in the top 25 in both career points and assists. James finished with 15 points and 13 assists, and the Cavs outscored the Magic by a whopping 29 points when he was on the floor.

13. LeBron on Robertson: "He's a guy who laid the foundation. I'm just trying to carry it on."

14. Magic coach Scott Skiles on James: "Every time there is a great young player, everybody always talks about Michael (Jordan) and stuff like that. But to me, he's always been more like a Magic (Johnson) or an Oscar-type player because of his vision. That's what makes him so difficult (to defend). … Give him a steady diet of running and double-teaming him or whatever, he's going to carve you up. He's going to hit everybody (with passes), find everybody, find the open man. … His vision certainly sets him apart from a lot of the great players."

15. Remember, this was Scott Skiles talking. And he still owns the NBA single-game assist record with 30. So the man knows a little something about great passing.

16. Blatt on LeBron joining Robertson: "That gives me chills to even hear that. That's an amazing, amazing accomplishment."

17. Finally, the Cavs (11-3) have won three straight and are doing it by posting up, cutting to the basket, finding the open man and as Love suggested, taking the best possible shot. Another really good test comes Wednesday, at talented Toronto.

NOVEMBER 26

Cavs need to fix late road issues

Six random dribbles on the Cavaliers' 103-99 loss to the host Toronto Raptors on Wednesday.

1. OK, we've found an early-season weakness for the Cavaliers. In their previous two road games, they played some of their worst basketball when it meant the most. Cause for concern? Well, yes, sure. Reason for widespread panic? Um, no. Not exactly. But if you're the Cavs and their fans, it can be maddening. And it cannot become a habit.

2. The Cavs looked exhausted in allowing an 82-all tie turn into a 9-2 run by the Raptors. In a pivotal stretch, the Cavs missed eight straight shots. And it seemed like every time you blinked, the Raptors were finishing another "and-one" opportunity. "If we're going to foul, we've got to make it count," Cavs center Tristan Thompson told reporters in Toronto.

3. Speaking of free throws, LeBron James (24 points) and Kevin Love (21 points, 13 rebounds) were the only two Cavs to attempt a shot from the line. Not for the fourth quarter — for the entire game. And Love was just 2-of-4. Worse, the Raptors buried the Cavs in the paint with a 52-28 scoring edge. That's just a lack of aggressiveness and settling for too many perimeter shots on the Cavs' end.

4. Coach David Blatt partially blamed some of the issues on fatigue, and that's entirely fair. The Cavs are still missing several major players — such as Kyrie Irving, Timofey Mozgov and Iman Shumpert. Matthew Dellavedova was also out with a sore calf, and if there's one guy who can keep the energy going in the fourth quarter, it's the relentless Delly.

5. Nonetheless, as James indicated after, this is a man's league and there's no room for excuses. "We have to have a bunker mentality when we go on the road," he said. "You gotta understand it's you guys vs. everyone else, vs. the fans, vs. the opposing group. Adversity is going to happen. We have to learn how to play on the road again, which we did last year."

6. LeBron makes a valid point. The Cavs (11-4) are unbeaten at home but just 3-4 in opposing gyms. They've lost to the Raptors, Bucks, Bulls and Pistons. The first three of those teams made the playoffs last season, and the Pistons look like they'll challenge this year. But each game was winnable. The Cavs are finishing off people at home. Clearly, they haven't done that with much consistency on the road. It's far from desperation time, but it's something that needs shored up.

NOVEMBER 29

LeBron saves Cavs' fairly dreary day

Random dribbles on the Cavaliers' squeaker of a 90-88 win over the visiting Brooklyn Nets on Saturday.

1. All that matters is the win. Especially when you consider the Cavs didn't

exactly play their best game of the season. Far from it actually — as they shot just 40 percent on the night.

2. The Cavs (13-4) were lumbering through their third game in four nights. The Nets (3-13) had been off since Wednesday. The Cavs also played and won a close game Friday at Charlotte. None of this is an excuse, because these Cavs should beat these Nets no matter when, where or how they meet. But they had tired legs and it showed.

3. That was especially the case in the first quarter, when the Cavs were a miserable 31 percent from the field. They missed easy shots, threw lazy passes and did a lot of standing around. And the defense wasn't much better.

4. If anything, winning this game is a real credit to the Cavs. They dug deep on an off night when it probably felt like they had nothing left. They made sure they didn't lose to an inferior opponent. The Nets were also a determined opponent. As LeBron James (26 points and the game-winner) told FOX Sports Ohio after, the Cavs will undoubtedly get every team's best shot.

5. How dire did it seem? Well, the Cavs trailed 83-76 with 4:40 left in the game. But they stayed with it and reclaimed the lead courtesy of an 8-0 run — spearheaded by You Know Who.

6. LeBron also buried two big free throws with 16 seconds remaining to put the Cavs up 88-85. Most nights in the NBA, the outcome is fairly determined at that point, the final moments becoming little more than a free-throw shooting contest.

7. Two things you definitely don't want to do in those situations: A). Give up a 3-pointer; B). Foul.

8. J.R. Smith pretty much did both — as Nets swingman Joe Johnson got Smith to leap into the air and commit a foul. Johnson was attempting a 3-pointer. That means he got three free throws. He made all three.

9. But the Cavs have LeBron James and no one else does. As you've certainly seen by now, James drove the lane and buried a running one-handed floater with a second left. Game over. For the ninth time in nine home games, Cavs win.

10. Kevin Love (26 points) had another outstanding night. He went 8-of-14

from the field, including 6-of-11 on threes. He basically was the entire offense in the third quarter. The Cavs were going through long droughts and settling for jumpers. Love, at least, was making his.

11. Mo Williams (14 points) also had another solid night, keeping the Cavs in it during the first half. Somewhat surprisingly, Williams didn't make a 3-pointer, missing his lone attempt. But per usual, he did a nice job from mid-range.

12. The Nets certainly don't seem as bad as their record. Brook Lopez (22 points, 10-of-15 shooting, nine rebounds) is an underrated center and as efficient as they come. Johnson (17 points) can still give them a lift from the perimeter and forward Thaddeus Young (16) always seems to give the Cavs fits. This is a veteran team with a good coach in Lionel Hollins — so I don't get it.

13. The Nets also lost to the undefeated Golden State Warriors on the road. And much like the Cavs, the Warriors struggled, before finally winning in overtime.

14. As Love told FOX Sports Ohio, it's a matter of resilience. "It's not always gonna be pretty," he said, and man he's right about that one.

15. But again, all that matters is the win. The Cavs did the necessary little things, even when things looked bleak, to pull it out. That included suffocating the Nets into 29 percent shooting in the fourth.

16. LeBron's shot was a little bit runner, a little bit baby hook. He said that was a first as far as game-winners go. "I've made layups, I've made pull-ups, obviously I've made step-back jumpers," he said. "I might go for the sky hook next time."

17. Finally, Cavs coach David Blatt smiled when talking about the night's final basket. "Yeah, just the way I drew it up," he said. "Yep. Give it to No. 23."

DECEMBER 4

Kyrie taking steps, draining Js

INDEPENDENCE, Ohio – Random dribbles on Kyrie Irving, the Cavaliers and the weekend ahead.

1. Irving and LeBron James stayed on the court well after practice, launching 3-pointers from various spots in what appeared to be a shooting competition. The two smiled, laughed and took part in some light-hearted trash talk before Irving met with the media.

2. Irving moved and shot the ball well. He participated in his first full practice of the year beforehand, making his long-range shooting game even more impressive. Irving smiled a lot when talking to reporters. You could just tell he was happy to be back.

3. Before you ask (actually, I'm sure you already have) — Irving has not revealed a return date. "Just taking it as it comes," he said, later adding that he's taken his "biggest steps" at practice this week.

4. I asked Irving how he was feeling, stamina-wise. He admitted he's still getting his wind back, but repeated he's coming along nicely in that area. And he sure looks A-OK to me. This is the second time in a week I've seen Kyrie go through shooting drills — and while that's a far cry from real game action, he's truly been lighting it up.

5. People always ask if I have a "gut feeling" when Irving will return. I don't. At all. And frankly, there's no rush. We're in early December. The only gut feeling I have is the Cavs' season won't end until June. That's a long way from December. While it's always fun to watch Irving, it's undoubtedly best to be patient in these situations.

6. Yes, Iman Shumpert is also getting closer to returning from wrist surgery. He too has been a practice participant this week. Like Irving, though, there is no official target date for Shumpert.

7. Now on to the Cavs who are healthy. They need to bounce back following a fairly flat performance in Tuesday's home loss to the Wizards. They also need to ignore the Pelicans' 4-15 record. Any home team with Anthony Davis is a threat.

8. After the one in New Orleans Friday, the Cavs have another toughie on the road vs. the Heat Saturday. LeBron and friends had their way against LeBron's old pals at The Q last month. So Dwyane Wade, Chris Bosh and the rest will be looking for revenge. But when it comes to the Cavs, what else is new, huh?

DECEMBER 5

LeBron soars, but Cavs dwindle

Random dribbles on the Cavaliers' 114-108 disappointment of an overtime defeat to the host Pelicans on Friday.

1. You can't get too worked up over one loss, especially since the Cavaliers have another chance to win Saturday night (at Miami). But this game should've been over when LeBron James hit two free throws to put the Cavs up by three in the final moments of regulation.

2. As Austin Carr said repeatedly on FOX Sports Ohio, the Cavs had one job: Do not let anyone on the Pelicans take a 3-pointer. So what did the Cavs do? They let Pelicans guard Jrue Holiday take a 3-pointer. And guess what? He made it.

3. Carr was clearly disgusted it even came to that, and you can't blame the man. The Cavs let an otherworldly performance from James (37 points) go to waste.

4. The Cavs (13-6) trailed by 13 points with less than 7 minutes remaining. Then James took over in amazing fashion. It was a basketball sight to behold — as he scored a whopping 24 points in the fourth quarter, most of which came off aggressive (and nifty) drives to the basket.

5. James' only notable miss came just before the final buzzer of regulation. He did everything right on his jumper from the wing. The ball just wouldn't cooperate.

6. Again, you're going to have nights like this in the NBA. The Cavs just can't make a habit of it. Frankly, they've had two in a row after losing to the Wizards at home Tuesday. This wasn't as bad as that one, but close. The Pelicans (5-15) are still finding themselves following injuries and a coaching change.

7. But as I warned beforehand (and you certainly already knew), no home team with Anthony Davis can be considered a joke. Davis lit up the Cavs' big men for 31 points, including a few biggies in overtime.

8. Still, that 3-pointer, man. How does that ever happen? This should've been over. And that's what will hurt until the Cavs tip off in Miami around 8 p.m.

9. Kevin Love added 15 points and 10 rebounds, but he's really struggling from beyond the arc. He was 0-of-5 on threes following an 0-of-3 performance Tuesday. He almost seemed too timid to shoot them in overtime, passing up a few decent looks. The Cavs will likely need a big night from Love vs. the Heat.

10. J.R. Smith scored 18, but he too was quiet later in the game. Timofey Mozgov added eight points on 4-of-5 shooting and eight rebounds, but didn't play again in the fourth, or in OT. It's hard to argue with Coach David Blatt's decisions, though. If the Cavs defend the three, they win. Blatt stressed that during a timeout before the play. The players just didn't execute.

11. Either way, again, it's not wise to get too bent out of shape over losses in early December. This thing is an absolute marathon. Odds are, no one will remember these games in May and June. Or for that matter, in January. You have to learn from it, move on, and get it right. As Kyrie Irving has been known to say, it's on to the next one.

DECEMBER 9

Getting tough lifts Cavs every time

CLEVELAND – Random dribbles on the Cavaliers' 105-100 win over the visiting Trail Blazers on Tuesday.

1. Even when the Cavaliers trailed by 18 points in the first half, I didn't count them out. In fact, I still sort of figured they would win. Damian Lillard, C.J. McCollum and the Blazers were red hot and I assumed that, eventually, their shooting would level off. Heck, even Blazers center Meyers Leonard hit a 3-pointer in the first half. Seriously. Meyers Leonard.

2. OK, so Lillard (33 points) and McCollum (24) never really did go cold. But the Cavs made them work much harder for their points in the final two

quarters. Part of it was the Blazers were making everything they threw up in the first half. Part of it was because the Cavs were letting them. It was a bad combination.

3. As an aside, wouldn't it be nice if every opponent the Cavs faced played something other than their absolute best game? I don't know if that's actually the case, but it sure feels that way. No doubt, going up against LeBron James — and the bright lights and TV ratings that come with it — clearly motivates people.

4. It's a lot different than playing, say, the Orlando Magic when no one is really watching. It's only human nature to go all out against the game's biggest names. So yes, King James and the Cavs end up getting everyone's best shot, every stinking minute of every stinking night. Still, few succeed.

5. As you know, the Cavs had lost three straight and James returned after a game of rest. You can read my quick game recap here. But just know LeBron looked completely refreshed on his way to 33 points and 10 rebounds.

6. Kevin Love also returned to form. He didn't rest Saturday's loss at Miami, but he sure didn't make much of an impact, either. This time, Love was much more aggressive, attacking the basket, drawing fouls and not settling for perimeter shots. In the end, Love scored 18 points and went 8-of-10 shooting on free throws.

7. As Cavs coach David Blatt said, the difference between Love's aggressiveness from last game to this was "noticeable."

8. More Blatt on Love: "Look, Kev is a critical player for us. We need him to play well and to play as hard as he did tonight. (He) was an important factor."

9. OK, two nitpicky concerns: Love is 0-of-13 on 3-pointers in his last four games combined. It's good he didn't just settle for jumpers, but the Cavs also need him to stretch the defense a little. He can't afford to lose confidence from the outside. He attempted only one shot from beyond the arc Tuesday.

10. The other nitpicky concern: Love finished with just four boards — and the Cavs were outrebounded by a 36-30 count. Granted, some of that had to do with Blatt's decision to go small (he started guard Jared Cunningham instead of center Timofey Mozgov in the second half). But some of it is the

Cavs just haven't been going after rebounds like they should.

11. That's not meant to pick on Love. Tristan Thompson was 1-of-3 shooting for two points and six rebounds. Mozgov played just 7 minutes and didn't score, didn't attempt a shot, didn't grab a rebound, didn't even commit a foul. Anderson Varejao played six minutes and didn't attempt a shot, either.

12. Read: The Cavs need more from their big men. There's no other way to spin it.

13. Frankly, it's a reason Blatt decided to go small. "We played the lineup that we had to play in order to win that game," he said. "That's what you gotta do sometimes. Maybe it's not exactly how you want to do it, or uncomfortable for somebody, but you gotta play to win."

14. Blatt said that after being asked a question about Mozgov. His take on Mozgov specifically: "He's just gotta keep working and keeping improving and get back to where he was."

15. Meanwhile, the guards and wings did indeed do their jobs. Matthew Dellavedova was his typical self by offering endless energy and contributing 7-of-12 shooting (including 3-of-5 on threes) for 17 important points. Cunningham scored 13 and did a nice job defensively.

16. The Cavs play just three more games in the next nine days — Friday, Tuesday and a week from Thursday. Despite winning just one of their previous four, they're 14-7 and remain in first place in the Eastern Conference. Sometime soon, I suspect, Kyrie Irving and Iman Shumpert will be back. And man, that could be all she wrote for the rest of the East.

3 THE ADDITION

DECEMBER 16

Cavs rolling, and here comes Kyrie

Eight random dribbles on the Cavaliers' 89-77 win at Boston on Tuesday.

1. This isn't true of everyone, but when the Cavs put their minds to it, they can accomplish just about anything. That's especially the case when you have LeBron James (24 points), and Kevin Love (20 and eight rebounds) is clicking.

2. The Cavs were contained and a little lifeless on their way to 40 points in the first half. Yes, 40 points. The Celtics are a determined team that plays intelligently and with energy. So they deserve some credit. But the Cavs just weren't creating many scoring opportunities off turnovers or shooting it very well.

3. That changed in the third quarter. The Cavs emerged from the locker room looking invigorated. They held the Celtics to 22 percent shooting over the next eight minutes. Timofey Mozgov was instrumental in that stretch. He played "big" the entire game, by clogging the lane and protecting the basket. James, Matthew Dellavedova and even J.R. Smith were also among those who helped turn things around defensively.

4. Of course, Iman Shumpert is always important in that area, too. He proved it again in his second game back from offseason wrist surgery. The bad news is Shumpert left in the second half with a groin injury. He never returned. Reports out of Boston said Shumpert is out for Thursday's home game vs. Oklahoma City. Reports also said the Cavs suspect the injury is not all that serious. We should know more Wednesday afternoon.

5. So make it three straight wins, including two straight on the road, and a 16-7 overall record. The Cavs also improved their road record to 6-6.

6. Ready for more good news? ESPN is reporting Kyrie Irving intends to make his season debut Thursday. As you know, Irving has been out since Game 1 of the Finals and underwent knee surgery in June.

7. Bottom line: This wasn't the prettiest game, but the Cavs turned a five-

point deficit into a 10-point advantage in about seven minutes. They never looked back against a well-coached and hungry opponent in the Celtics (14-11).

8. LeBron on the win: "We knew it was going to be that type of game, just coming off the playoff series we had with them (a 4-0 series sweep by the Cavs). And, it's our first time seeing them. We were able to answer the call."

DECEMBER 18

Slim at guard, Cavs pass a toughie

Random dribbles on the Cavaliers' 104-100 win over the visiting Thunder on Thursday.

1. Who needs guards when you have LeBron James? After all, along with 33 points and nine rebounds, James took care of the passing — finishing with a game-high 11 assists.

2. Simply put, it was James who set the tone for the stronger ball movement in the fourth quarter. And that's a big reason why the Cavs were able to come back and snap OKC's six-game winning streak.

3. That's not a shot at Cavs guards Matthew Dellavedova (who hit several key 3-pointers and had 10 assists of his own), or J.R.Smith (11 points). Even Jared Cunningham contributed to the backcourt off the bench, adding some strong defense and finishing 3-of-4 from the floor.

4. It's just that the Cavs were without Mo Williams (right thumb injury), and once again, Iman Shumpert (groin), and still, Kyrie Irving (knee). So they were down three men who could help try to manage Thunder point man Russell Westbrook. Facing a team that also has Kevin Durant, well, for a while it looked like a lost cause.

5. Westbrook finished with 27 points and 10 assists. Durant had 25 points. The Thunder were in control for much of the second half. Then Kevin Love knocked down a 3-pointer while getting fouled. Then Love threw a pinpoint outlet pass to James for a layup. Then the Cavs built a 10-point lead, and held on during the frantic final three minutes.

6. So Love (11 points, seven boards) certainly had some moments. Same goes for Tristan Thompson (12 points, 15 rebounds, tons of alley-oop

dunks). Also, Richard Jefferson had 13 points, making 3-of-6 threes. Dellavedova scored 11.

7. Basically, this was the type of total-team effort the Cavs (17-7) needed against a quality opponent such as the Thunder (17-9). So make it four straight wins for Cleveland — now 11-1 at home.

8. James dove for a loose ball in the fourth quarter and crashed into stands, and into the wife of golfer Jason Day. It was a scary moment for sure. Ellie Day is said to be doing fine.

9. Cavs coach David Blatt on courtside seats: "It's always concerned me, the sideline seats. Always concerned me, because things like that, when you're talking about players of this speed and physicality and effort level, it's not a simple thing.The powers that be are the ones that really need to decide how to deal with that. He made an honest attempt at the basketball, that's all, obviously. We all hope she's OK."

10. The Thunder have lost. The 76ers and Knicks, both at home, are up next. So yes, it's quite possible the Cavs could own the NBA's longest winning streak heading into their Finals rematch at the Warriors on Christmas Day. The Bulls are the only other team riding a four-game winning streak entering Friday.

11. And yes, it is also quite possible Irving could make his season debut Sunday vs. the Sixers. If so, he has told fans he will be the one to break the news.

DECEMBER 21

Kyrie returns, and Cavs take on new life

CLEVELAND — Random dribbles on the Cavaliers' 108-86 win over the visiting 76ers on Sunday.

1. It's hard to get a sense of much of anything when you're playing the Sixers. They're just so bad. But Kyrie Irving did make his season debut, and the Cavaliers did cruise. So everyone at Quicken Loans Arena went home happy.

2. Irving's first half described in a word: Rusty. Irving's second half: Promising. Actually, Irving looked just short of all the way back in the

game's final 24 minutes – after scoring two points on 1-of-6 shooting in the first.

3. His final line: 12 points, 5-of-12 shooting, 2-of-2 on 3-pointers, four assists, two steals and just one turnover in 17 minutes. This was little more than a glorified practice game, but even so, Irving easily passed his first test.

4. Kyrie on his day: "Kind of been a long, long road, but finally getting out there with my teammates was a pleasure."

5. Irving missed his first layup. He admitted he was kind of caught off guard by how wide open he was at the rim. After the game, LeBron James shouted across the locker room to take a playful jab at Irving for that very play. "As you can hear, I did trick the first layup but it's OK," Irving said. "I'm not worried. It feels good, just getting this one out of the way."

6. Of course, it was James who had an opportunity for a fast-break dunk, but instead flipped the ball ahead to Irving for a layup – which resulted in Irving's first basket. "He had missed his first couple shots and I was like the best way to come back is to get a layup, get an easy one," James said, "and it was only right I was able to find him, welcoming him back the best way I know how."

7. Mostly, the Cavs are near back to full strength, which is bad news for the rest of the league. "We're almost there," James said. The Cavs were clearly inspired by having Irving back on the floor. They know how good they were last year when he played.

8. James finished with a game-high 23 points on 10-of-17 shooting. Matthew Dellavedova was again fantastic in terms of effort, and more recently, real stats to back it up. Delly, who returned to his reserve role behind Irving, went for 20 points on 7-of-10 from the floor. That included 4-of-7 on threes. You can just see how starting in the Finals has done wonders for Dellavedova's confidence.

9. Kevin Love only took four shots and scored just 10 points — but he was also only needed for 22 minutes. You could call it a slow night, but again, the Cavs were playing the Sixers. It's hard to take games like this too seriously.

10. I could go on and on about how much damage Sixers GM Sam Hinkie has done to the league's overall product by willingly building a culture of losing for his franchise. I won't, but only because I'm a fan of Sixers coach

Brett Brown, and new associate coach Mike D'Antoni, and Jerry Colangelo, who was just hired to run the team. Those guys will at least get this to something beyond a laughable level soon.

11. The Knicks visit Cleveland on Wednesday, and they will give us a better idea of how things really are. All we can go on now is the Cavs (18-7) have won five straight and Kyrie is back. Hard to find any bad news with that, huh?

DECEMBER 22

Numbers explain why Cavs rolling

Random dribbles on the Cavaliers, who have won five straight entering Wednesday's home game against the Knicks.

1. A quick look at the numbers shows why the Cavs have been playing so well lately. And not surprisingly, it starts with defense.

2. The Cavs are limiting opponents to 95.6 points per game. That's third-best in the NBA. Only the Spurs (allowing 88.9 ppg) and the Heat (94.9) are doing better on D.

3. They're scoring 101.8 per game — tied for 13th (with the Pistons). That stat should increase now that Kyrie Irving is back. Especially if Matthew Dellavedova keeps scoring 20 a game, as he did Monday vs. the 76ers.

4. That's a joke about Delly. The Cavs don't need him to score 20. Or even 10, for that matter. But the point is this: Along with the Big Three of LeBron James, Kevin Love and Irving, there are a lot of guys on this team capable of making shots and finding ways to score. That includes everyone from Dellavedova to J.R. Smith to Iman Shumpert and Mo Williams (once he returns from a thumb injury). And those are just the guards.

5. Another credit to the backcourt (and James): The Cavs are seventh in the NBA in assists at 23 per game. As for the frontcourt, Tristan Thompson, Timofey Mozgov and the rest deserve credit for their work on the boards. The Cavs are eighth in the NBA in rebounding at 44.8 a night.

6. Of course, coach David Blatt and his staff also warrant mention for all of this. Blatt managed to keep this team motivated and playing well as it waited for Irving to return, and suffered (yet again) through some key injuries and

a couple of lulls.

7. Interestingly, we aren't hearing the rumors or rumblings about Blatt this season. Remember last year, when everyone was talking about lead assistant Tyronn Lue all the time? I'll be honest, I forgot Lue was even part of the staff this year. And I mean that in a good way, as the national media just can't seem to drum up any drama. Thank goodness for that one.

8. I did look at the sidelines the other day and marvel over the assistants — reminding myself that Lue is considered The NBA's Next Really Good Head Coach, and that Larry Drew and Jim Boylan are still sitting next to Blatt. Both Drew and Boylan did nice jobs in their own head-coaching stints.

9. Of course, the biggie with the Warriors (and Christmas Day) is almost here. Fans league-wide can't wait. But remember, it's not even the middle of the regular season. Win or lose, it's no time to get all up in arms over anything. That said, I know 99.37652 percent of the people reading this column think it would sure be awesome if the Cavs won.

DECEMBER 24

Cavs throw ugly punch, but hey, it's a win

Random dribbles on the Cavaliers' 91-84 win over the visiting Knicks on Tuesday.

1. It was the first time the Cavs had their entire lineup healthy and active all season. And it didn't really show — as they had to sort of slug their way to a win over a Knicks team that was missing Carmelo Anthony (sprained ankle) and playing on the road.

2. Hard to blame the Cavs, though. Christmas and the Golden State Warriors are next. They may have been thinking about that a little. Plus, the Cavs can beat the Knicks in Cleveland on cruise control. I'm not implying that they gave half-effort on purpose. But sometimes, when you know you only need to flip a switch to beat a team … well, it makes waiting around and flipping that switch an easy thing to do. If that makes any sense.

3. Either way, you can't criticize a team for getting a victory. The Cavs just weren't in sync offensively. That can happen when your rotations change and star players such as Kyrie Irving are still trying to find their rhythm. A

win is a win, though, and the Cavs (19-7) have won six straight. The business of pro basketball is pretty black and white. The Cavs did their job.

4. LeBron James, of course, led the way when it came to delivering at the end. He scored seven of his 24 points down the stretch — and the defense did the rest. The Knicks held an 82-80 edge with 4:07 left. They scored just one more basket the rest of the way.

5. James on the game: "We preach offensively it's not always going to be pretty. Tonight we needed the defensive end. We just got stops."

6. Kevin Love was magnificent with 23 points and 13 rebounds. Tristan Thompson went for an underrated 10 and 14, respectively, off the bench. That included 6-of-6 shooting on free throws. And Matthew Dellavedova played another strong floor game with seven assists – one of which resulted in a big basket from James to put the Cavs ahead for good.

7. I've been extremely impressed with Knicks rookie Kristaps Porzingis (23 points, 13 boards). The guy is 7-foot-3 and shoots like a guard. He's also athletic and mentally tough enough to do the dirty work near the basket. He's a major reason why the Knicks (14-16) have made strides this season. Read: I don't want to be facing the guy once he finally learns the ins and outs of the NBA.

8. Not much more to say on this one. All of the focus now turns to the Warriors, who improved to 27-1 after Tuesday's blowout win over Utah. The Cavs look better than they did at this point last season — but the defending champs do, too. It's worth noting that the Warriors are 13-0 at home.

9. Final thoughts: The Cavs have the talent, depth and firepower to beat anyone in the league, anywhere and anytime. But they will need to put it all together, and I mean for the entire 48 minutes. It's been a long time since an NBA team has been able to capitalize on other people's mistakes like the Warriors. And I mean a *long* time. They can deflate you faster than you can say, "Steph Curry for 3."

DECEMBER 26

Still too early to fret over Cavs' loss

Random dribbles on the Cavaliers' 89-83 defeat to the host Warriors on Friday.

1. Let's be honest, neither team exemplified what you'd expect to see from world champions. No one will admit it, but perhaps both groups were a little tight. And you know what? That's OK. It truly was the first "big game" of the regular season for everyone involved.

2. Despite the buzz, there's really not much to take away from this one. I mean, the Wizards played better vs. the Cavs than the Warriors — as the Wizards never trailed in handing the Cavs their lone home loss a few weeks back. Does that mean the Wizards are better than the Warriors? Um, no. But it does mean, again, we shouldn't read too much into anything right now.

3. LeBron James was fairly upbeat after the game and I can't say I blame him. The Cavs became the first opponent to hold the Warriors to less than 90 points at home since 2013. That's not to say they should be excited about losing – but they slowed a team that prides itself on not getting slowed, and gave themselves a shot to win on the road.

4. Then again, when it came to shots, the Cavs (19-8) couldn't make a one. At least, not a meaningful one. Not much of any one, for that matter. They finished a miserable 31 percent from the floor, including less than 17 percent on 3-pointers. Basically, when the Cavs lined up to shoot, the rim cringed with fear. The Warriors had something to do with that, no doubt. The Cavs had something to do with it, too.

5. Kevin Love went 5-of-16 and 0-of-5 on threes. For Kyrie Irving, it was 4-of-15 and 0-of-6. Even LeBron struggled mightily — by shooting 10-of-26 and 1-of-5 from beyond the arc. He also missed a couple of big free throws near the end.

6. Love on the misses: "It's one of those nights. I don't know if you'll ever see Kyrie and myself go 0-of-11 from three again."

7. It's too bad, because the Cavs did an excellent job defensively. On top of limiting the Warriors to less than 100 at home for the first time in 48 regular-season games, the Cavs held Warriors guard Steph Curry to 19

points. Curry entered the game as the NBA's leading scorer, erupting for an incredible 31 points a night.

8. Anyway, as LeBron said: "We play like that defensively, we're going to be a very tough team to beat."

9. James finished with 25 points and nine rebounds, but had just two assists. Love went for 10 points and 18 boards. Irving finished with 13 points. J.R.Smith, who actually shot the ball well, scored 14. And Matthew Dellavedova had a solid game off the bench with 10 points and five rebounds.

10. Still, it's pretty evident that coach David Blatt's club is a little out of sync following the returns of Irving and Iman Shumpert (scoreless on 0-of-6 shooting). That's completely understandable.

11. LeBron on the state of things: "It's an adjustment period. It's not going to just happen — you plug a guy in here, plug two guys in there, and it automatically happens. It's going to be an adjustment period. But we'll be fine. We'll be fine toward February and March."

12. This isn't intended to downplay the Warriors. They're 28-1 and that's flat-out remarkable, no matter how you try to spin it. They certainly didn't play their best here, either. But I predicted the Cavs would lose, and I predict the Warriors will lose when they come to Cleveland on Jan. 18. And guess what? It still won't be a big deal.

13. My point? Well, LeBron is right. We're not even at the midpoint of the season. The Cavs are clearly still finding their way. That's not to say they'll be the best team in the league when they do. But I bet they'll be a whole lot better than they were Friday.

14. One thing's for sure: They have to find a way to get Timofey Mozgov going on a much more regular basis. He hurt his team vs. the Warriors — and not just because he failed to score (0-of-5 shooting). He wasn't aggressive, he wasn't intimidating and he made too many silly mistakes on both ends. Mozgov is an important piece and the Cavs believe in him. But his confidence seems shaky right now. The Cavs need for that to change.

15. Final word from Kyrie: "We had different lineups that we're not used to yet. It's going to take us some time before we start clicking on all cylinders. When we do, I mean … it's going to be scary."

DECEMBER 27

Time for Cavs to face, correct issues

Random dribbles on the Cavaliers' 105-76 embarrassment of a loss to the host Trail Blazers on Saturday.

1. Won't be going overboard on this one. I mean, what really is there to say? This is a very unofficial opinion, but that was likely the worst loss since LeBron James returned to the team more than a year ago. So no need to keep reliving it.

2. As LeBron said afterward: "Throw it in the trash. There was nothing we did good tonight."

3. And Cavs fans all across the land gave a hearty amen.

4. I tend not to put too much into one game, good or bad. Strange occurrences can happen during the course of an 82-game season. It's good to not get too high or too low until the games really, really mean something. That said, the Cavs have displayed some troubling signs during the past week.

5. For one, they have lost two straight. This one came a night after the 89-83 defeat at the hands of the Warriors — and the 76- and 83-point outputs are season lows.

6. Read: What on earth is wrong with the offense? With as many weapons as this team has, there is simply no excuse.

7. In the past three games combined (including Wednesday's win over the Knicks), the Cavs are averaging 83 points per game. They are shooting a miserable 36 percent from the floor, and just 26 percent on 3-pointers.

8. Again, no excuse for that. I've been covering this game for a long time — and I cannot believe an ENTIRE TEAM of professional athletes can go into a shooting slump at the same time. High schoolers? Sure. College players? Absolutely. The pros? Well, it may happen for a game, where not a soul can get a thing to fall. That's what is called a fluke. But when it happens three straight games, well, that's a trend. And it's one the Cavs need to break.

9. When shots don't fall game after game after game, the biggest issue is likely ball movement and player movement. Guys aren't getting the ball in good spots, and part of the reason is because they aren't MOVING to good spots. Another reason is because once they get to those good spots, no one is passing them the ball.

10. Again, to quote LeBron: "Offensively, we are in a funk right now."

11. And Cavs fans all across the land gave a hearty amen.

12. James finished with just 12 points on 4-of-13 shooting. But at least he only played 28 minutes. Still, the Blazers outscored the Cavs by 29 points when James was on the floor. That was the worst "plus-minus" rating on the team. I occasionally check Twitter, and LeBron is really hearing it from the fans. He's not entirely to blame, but he hasn't been himself lately.

13. Kevin Love scored 13 to lead the Cavs (19-9). Kyrie Irving took the night off to rest. Many of his teammates weren't far behind. Matthew Dellavedova and Richard Jefferson (10 points apiece) were the only other Cavs to score in double figures.

14. Meanwhile, the Cavs allowed little-known Blazers swingman Allen Crabbe to go nuts to the tune of 26 points. The Blazers shot 41 percent on 3-pointers. Oh, by the way, their best player, point guard Damian Lillard, missed the game with a bum foot. And the hits just keep on coming, don't they?

15. But again, you can't get too worked up over one game in late December. As analyst Austin Carr suggested on the FOX Sports Ohio broadcast, the Cavs need to just forget about it and play like champions in the next one. That takes place Monday in Phoenix.

16. As for Cavs coach David Blatt, well, you can't lose faith in a guy after three bad games. You can, however, wonder if all the healthy bodies are causing some rotations that lack chemistry. Blatt needs to get that figured out here soon. On the bright side, he has plenty of time. Man oh man, there is so much time.

17. Blatt on the loss: "We're not a bad team all of a sudden. ... This was a bad night. Plain and simple."

18. I tend to agree with the coach. Let's see how the Cavs respond. As Carr suggested, bounce-back opportunities are often where true title contenders

show themselves. So … Panicked? No. Worried? Maybe, but just a little. Anxious to see how the Cavs get this fixed? Oh, you'd better believe it.

DECEMBER 29

Cavs closer to Kyrie's 'scary' promise

Random dribbles on the Cavaliers' 101-97 victory over the host Suns on Monday.

1. Kyrie Irving may have committed his favorite mistake. In case you missed it, Irving nearly threw the ball away late in the game and the Cavs clinging to a 96-95 lead. It looked as if Irving thought LeBron James would cut to the basket. James didn't cut. Kyrie passed to the middle of the key anyway.

2. Just when you thought, "OH NO!" J.R. Smith came out of nowhere, running from the corner to save the day. He grabbed the errant pass. He threw it to Kevin Love outside the 3-point line. Love bobbled the ball. It looked like he might lose it. He appeared to think about shooting – but he was closely guarded. The shot clock was winding down. So Love passed to Irving out top.

3. With nothing left to do, Irving shot it. He was way beyond the 3-point line. Money. Cavs win. Kyrie is back.

4. A game off may have served Irving well. In the event you forgot, he rested for the debacle in Portland, where the Cavs got blitzed by the Trail Blazers. He looked refreshed vs. the Suns – scoring a season-high 22 points on 7-of-16 shooting. He also hit a floater in the lane before his big three. That gave the Cavs a 96-92 edge. Irving played 24 minutes.

5. Kyrie smiled as he told FOX Sports Ohio about his late errant pass, and the 3-pointer that eventually resulted. "Probably one of the ugliest possessions of my career right there," he said.

6. Meanwhile, LeBron had an "off" night with 14 points on 4-of-10 from the floor. It's probably why he sounded relieved when speaking of Irving's return. "It's a great feeling having the kid back," James said. "He does so much for our team."

7. Something Irving said after the loss to the Warriors on Christmas Day

has stuck with me. "It's going to take us some time before we start clicking on all cylinders," he said. "When we do, I mean ... it's going to be scary."

8. Smith added 17 points, Love scored 16 and Tristan Thompson collected 10 rebounds while starting for Timofey Mozgov. Cavs coach David Blatt indicated that he is likely to stick with Thompson as the starter for the foreseeable future.

9. Blatt on the final moments: "J.R. Smith made an incredible winning play to save that ball. That ball was going out of bounds and it looked like it would be their possession. He made a fabulous save. Kyrie made a huge shot."

10. The Cavs (20-9) can barely celebrate, as they travel to Denver to face the Nuggets on Tuesday night. Irving is expected to rest. He says it's the final time he will do so on a back-to-back.

11. Either way, the Cavs needed this win after two straight losses. It wasn't a masterpiece. But here's a newsflash: They're not all going to be. What matters is they win some road games while getting their rotations figured out and their rhythms back. They managed to pull that off Monday.

DECEMBER 30

Issues for Cavs? It's all hot air

Random dribbles on the Cavaliers' 93-87 win over the host Nuggets on Tuesday.

1. Second game in two nights. Thin air. No Kyrie Irving. A Nuggets team that isn't always as bad as we think. Yet all night, it seemed like the Cavs were in complete control.

2. This probably wasn't LeBron James' best game of the season — but it was up there. James is turning 31 years old. He scored 34 points. He threw down some serious dunks. He made a couple of cool steals. He looked as energized as any other time this season. It's worth noting James did all this on the last stop out West. The Cavs finished the trip 2-2.

3. Did the Cavs look like world-beaters on their Western swing? Nah. Not really. But even when they're less-than-stellar, they still look plenty capable of beating anyone in a seven-game series. For now, that's good enough.

4. I know. Some fans want the Cavs to look like champions in late December. Some fans want them to dominate like the Warriors have on their way to a 29-1 start. But I wonder if those fans remember the 61- and 66-win seasons of the first LeBron era. I wonder if those fans remember how those seasons ended.

5. Last year, the Cavs started 19-20. They reached the Finals without Kevin Love. They played the firat game with Irving on one good knee, then five more Finals games without him at all. Read: It's important to remain focused on the biggest of all goals.

6. Anyway, I've written and said all that before, and I'm sure I will again — the message being to appreciate this team. I sure do. The Cavs don't always play exactly how I'd like them to play. They're not perfect on every possession. They sometimes do silly things I haven't seen since my old rec-league games vs. The Beer Keg Lounge Lizards.

7. But the Cavs are 21-9 and clearly, the rest of the East must go through Cleveland. Frankly, I don't think it can, and frankly, neither do you. As for the West, I'll say this: Sorry, but still not afraid. The Cavs finished last regular season 34-3 when healthy. They're better this year.

8. OK, back to the Nuggets game. Irving rested on the second night of a back-to-back. That makes sense at this time of year. He says he doesn't want to do it again. But I won't blame Irving or the Cavs if it happens. Once things get easier (and they likely will), there's no harm in letting guys get their legs ready for the biggies in April, May and June.

9. Love scored eight points and grabbed 14 rebounds. I'd like to see Love get his scoring back up. The one way he can do that is to shoot the ball better. He struggled on this trip and finished 4-of-16 from the floor Tuesday. That included 0-of-5 on 3-pointers. Again, plenty of time to rediscover the touch. So again, not overly worried.

10. Overall, the Cavs were just 4-of-22 on threes. Don't know if it was the four-games-in-five nights or what, but this must change. Thankfully, the Cavs are off until Saturday (at home vs. the Magic). They could use the rest and some time to get their jumpers back in order.

11. Cavs coach David Blatt on the win: "We wanted and felt that we needed to finish this trip strong, to get a couple of wins, to go into the new year with good momentum and a good feeling."

12. LeBron had fun with the whole concept of Denver's thin air. Nobody seemed all that winded, except for maybe the final 35 seconds. "When the air is thick, it kind of holds me back a little bit when I jump," James joked.

13. Former Cavs update: Mike Miller went scoreless in seven minutes and J.J. Hickson never got off the bench for the Nuggets (12-20). Miller visited with his former Cavs teammates before tipoff. Same goes for Cavs center Timofey Mozgov and his ex-Nuggets teammates. Nuggets coach Mike Malone, who spent five years as a Cavs assistant, also said hello to LeBron and some of the guys.

4 STARS ALIGNING

JANUARY 5

Kyrie, Cavs display strength and unity

CLEVELAND — Random dribbles from the Cavaliers' 122-100 win over the visiting Raptors on Monday.

1. Believe it or not, this was just a two-point game at halftime. Then the Cavs turned up the D (they've been doing that a lot lately) and the Raptors sort of fell apart (they've done that a little lately, too). The two are often related.

2. Entering Monday, the Cavs had limited opponents to 88 points and 40 percent shooting over the past 10 games. That included just 29 percent on 3-pointers. But the Raptors came out on fire. Actually, both teams were shooting around 60 percent (and 50 percent on threes) for most of the first half.

3. I don't want to overwhelm you with numbers, but just know the Raptors finished 49 percent shooting overall and 41 percent from beyond the arc. So it wasn't the Cavs' finest defensive effort of the season — but in the second half, it was pretty doggone good.

4. Defense aside, if Kyrie Irving (25 points, eight assists, six rebounds) is anywhere near this good on a regular basis again (I suspect he will be), the Cavs are going to be extremely tough to beat in a seven-game series. I don't care who you are.

5. The Cavs (23-9) now lead the Raptors (21-15) by four games in the Eastern Conference. A lot of folks believe the Raptors are the East's second-best team — and will fight for that spot all season with the Bulls, Heat, Hawks and maybe Pacers. Clearly, though, the Cavs came into this game wanting to show everybody who's the real No. 1.

6. Irving to FOX Sports Ohio: "We wanted to try to make a statement. Not just to ourselves, but to the rest of the league."

7. I'm pretty certain this is the longest it's ever taken me to mention LeBron James (20 points, 7-of-11 shooting, seven assists). Then again, think about

this: He wasn't even needed in the fourth quarter of a game against one of the East's elite. That's how well things went in the second half.

8. And let's not forget J.R. Smith, who erupted for 24 points in his best all-around showing of the season. Like I've written before, Smith just seems to play so much more relaxed, and get so many more good looks at the basket, when Irving is healthy and at his best.

9. Every Cavs starter scored in double figures. Along with Irving, Smith and James, Kevin Love and Tristan Thompson went for 14 apiece. Thompson grabbed 11 rebounds, Love had nine.

10. Thompson gave a fine effort, no doubt. But you also have to love how the Cavs immediately went on a 16-2 run when Timofey Mozgov checked in for Thompson in the third quarter. It's important for Mozgov to feel comfortable in the season's second half. The Cavs desperately need his defense at the rim.

11. LeBron on Kyrie: "'He's much better than an All-Star. If he continues to play the way he's been playing, but also progress in his game over the years, he can do something that's very special. I know in my head what he can become and tonight he showed it."

12. Irving exchanged hugs with James and Cavs coach David Blatt after the game. You can just tell the other guys enjoy seeing their star point guard return to top-notch form following knee surgery.

13. Matthew Dellavedova scored 11 points off the bench and bounced back nicely after committing a couple early turnovers.

14. One of my favorite moments of the night took place after Delly turned the ball over a second time and Blatt subbed him out. Delly returned to the bench, took a seat, threw a towel, and was clearly frustrated with himself. Then veteran guard Mo Williams put his arm around Dellavedova and offered what was clearly some calming support.

15. Dellavedova is getting most of the reserve point guard minutes behind Irving — as opposed to Williams. Yet it was no less than Williams who was the first to encourage his younger teammate. Just one example that this is a tight-knit and very united group.

16. The Cavs now play seven of eight on the road. The lone home game in that stretch? Try the defending champion Warriors, on Jan. 18. Also, both

of the Cavs' games vs. the Spurs take place in January. Should be an interesting month.

JANUARY 7

Cavs show whose stars are brightest

Random dribbles on the Cavaliers' 121-115 win over the host Wizards on Wednesday.

1. This was a game the Cavaliers really wanted, and they turned to their brightest stars to make sure it happened. It's really that simple.

2. The Wizards are responsible for the lone blemish on the Cavs' 15-1 home record. As LeBron James indicated beforehand, the Cavs owed them one. They also wanted to begin their six-game road swing on a high note. So after a rather vanilla first quarter, the Cavs turned it on.

3. Then they turned it up early in the third, when James went bananas. The best play of the night may have been when Wizards forward Otto Porter defended LeBron tightly outside the 3-point arc on the baseline. Porter was right in James' mug, waving his arms, being aggressive and making sure James didn't take a jumper. Well, guess what? Big mistake.

4. LeBron simply put the ball on the floor, took a huge first step, got past Porter and went in for a monster two-handed slam — slapping the backboard on his return to Earth. It was a statement dunk that seemed to say, "Hey, kid. Don't play me close."

5. Of course, Irving put together a few nifty moves of his own in the fourth quarter after the Wizards closed an 18-point deficit to, like, nothing. It's truly amazing how quickly Kyrie has come around after knee surgery in June. LeBron finished with 34 points. Kyrie had 32 — including 10 in a row (and 21 overall) in the final eight minutes.

6. I wrote it before and I'll write it again and again. When LeBron and Kyrie are healthy and playing their best, the Cavs are the team to beat in this league. I really don't care if you're 33-2 or whatever.

7. I've also written this before (and even tweeted it Wednesday): But J.R. Smith is just so much more carefree and effective alongside a healthy Irving. Smith finished with 25 points on 10-of-16 shooting. With Irving,

James and Kevin Love (eight points, nine rebounds) out there, Smith has zero pressure to score. With no pressure, Smith doesn't need to be tight when it comes to shooting from the perimeter.

8. This looked like a game straight out of the old American Basketball Association, and that's OK. The Cavs (24-9) can win that way, provided they get stops when things are tight. They did that Wednesday. But man, what a far cry this game was from the Christmas Day slugfest vs. the Warriors.

9. Smith on Kyrie: "To do what he's doing, nine or 10 months to get back, and still be able to come out there and shake and bake ... it's remarkable."

10. Amen to that.

11. Kyrie on Kyrie: "'The first few games were just being able to solidify myself back in the league and being an elite athlete and get around guards. That was the hump I needed to get over, and now I think I'm starting to get over it going from game to game."

12. Now for a couple of nitpicks. Again, no concerns with the pace at which this game was played. But the Cavs still too often get caught watching LeBron (and now, Kyrie) and standing in place. They can make things a lot easier on themselves — and are truly at their absolute best — when things are moving.

13. Case in point: The Cavs compiled just 16 assists, compared to 31 for the Wizards. And the Wizards' rally was almost solely a result of the Cavs dribbling, dribbling and dribbling some more, then firing up a desperation heave near the end of the shot clock. It worked Wednesday. But it's not a long-term solution.

14. Nitpick No. 2: Love took just 10 shots and the bench scored a measly 10 points. Also, LeBron played 40 minutes. The Cavs are deeper and more well-balanced than those numbers would indicate. This was an exciting game and the Cavs won. That's the bottom line. But when talking about the big picture, the Cavs will need to be more than just a two-man show. Because, frankly, they are.

15. OK, now that we got that nonsense out of the way, here's Cavs coach David Blatt on Kyrie: "It's only reasonable to expect that he's going to go through a process and still have days when he's better and days when he's going to have some effect of the many months that he was out. But it sure

didn't look like that tonight."

16. Wizards guard John Wall (20 points, 12 assists, 4-of-4 on threes) is a fine player and his team will likely rebound from its 15-18 start. But he shouldn't have complained about the All-Star voting. By the time the actual game gets here, everyone will know that Irving deserves to start.

JANUARY 9

Healthy Cavs now winning by committee

Random dribbles on the Cavaliers, who have won six straight after Friday's 125-99 hammer job of the host Timberwolves.

1. Never once did I feel the Cavs were threatened, even when they refused to defend Andrew Wiggins early in the game. The Wolves may be good someday. But boy, they sure are bad now.

2. The Cavs (25-9) played hard only when they needed to and still won by 26. They could've gone for 140 and held Minnesota to 75 had they treated this like a finals game. And that's not another shot at the Wolves. It just goes to show the Cavs are really clicking and have the potential to bury you quickly.

3. Amazingly, LeBron James was held to 13. Or more accurately, James never forced a thing and decided 13 points was all the Cavs needed. He was right. Kyrie Irving also scored just 13. Each man went 5-of-12 from the field. Nice to have those normal-human types of nights from your best players and still win by 26.

4. So who made it all happen? Well, everyone. It really was a total team effort and that too says a lot about the Cavs. The Wolves were so overmatched this resembled a scrimmage. Yet the Cavs never allowed it to turn into a one-on-one contest where they only looked for their own shots.

5. J.R. Smith went for 27 points on a sizzling 10-of-12 shooting. As I've mentioned 157 times, his rise just happens to coincide with Irving's return to full health. It's no coincidence.

6. Is it too confusing for me to use "coincide" and "coincidence" in the same sentence? If so, just know Smith has been really good lately. So has Irving. They play well together, and Smith plays very well off Kyrie.

7. Smith last season when Irving wasn't healthy: 11.2 points on 37 percent shooting. Smith when Irving played: 12.7 points on 43 percent. So far, J.R. is taking an even bigger leap next to Irving.

8. Is it just me, or has watching this team been a lot more fun lately, too? Even when the Cavs aren't at their best, they're never really bad. They may lose a few here and there, but it's hard to find any red flags. That's a good sign when you still have more than half a regular season (and all the playoffs) to go.

9. Kevin Love was excellent with 20 points and nine rebounds. I liked how he fought to overcome his continued shooting woes. It's OK if the ball doesn't go in the basket. Get tough, do the dirty work and find ways to help your team win by any means necessary. On Friday, that was Love.

10. Wiggins had his usual monster scoring game vs. the Cavs with 35 points. He finished 12-of-19 shooting. He even doubled his assist average with a whopping three (which is a lot for him). I'm not ripping Wiggins, because he's a fine a talent. But he basically shot the ball every time he touched it and took his team out of the game. He's a young player who has a long way to go when it comes to learning how to win.

11. I was, however, immensely impressed with No. 1 overall pick Karl-Anthony Towns (22 points, 11-of-14 shooting). The Wolves' rookie center is a player, period. He actually looked to move the ball and try to win the game, passing for three assists and setting up some other wide-open shots that missed. He's gonna be a major force in this league soon.

12. Love on the rise of Smith: "It is nice. A lot of different guys can carry the load on this team. It's not just one or two guys and that makes for a pretty formidable group."

13. Smith on Smith: "When I catch the ball, nobody's coming to help. Nobody's coming. It's just me and my man on an island, so I can pretty much do what I want. But nine times out of 10 the catch-and-shoot is already open and that's when I'm at my best."

14. Iman Shumpert also had a huge night with 23 points, and Matthew Dellavedova added an underrated 10. Even Timofey Mozgov looked good with seven points and nine boards in 24 minutes. James added 12 rebounds and eight assists.

15. Interestingly, James and Irving and Smith were the big guns in the previous win vs. the Wizards. On Friday, it was Smith and Shumpert and Love. So re-read Love's comments in Dribble No. 12. The Cavs really are winning by committee.

JANUARY 11

Another Cavs win more than enough

Random dribbles on the Cavaliers' admirable (yes, admirable) 95-85 win over the host 76ers on Sunday.

1. It wasn't always pretty and the Cavaliers finally failed to score 120 points. But it's never easy to beat a team four times in a season — as the Cavs have now done to the Sixers. That's especially the case when a team is hungry and improving — as the Sixers are.

2. Sometimes, fans and reporters covering a team (and even members of the team) feel inclined to criticize when said team doesn't beat an inferior opponent by 40. Sometimes, it's tough to tip your hat to the other guy. But the Sixers deserve credit here. They're playing spirited basketball lately. They defended and slowed the pace.

3. Still, it's the Cavs who have LeBron James. One game after not forcing a thing and scoring 13 points, he put the team on his back and tied his season high with 37. He was 15-of-22 from the floor. He passed for nine assists. He grabbed seven rebounds. He did the dirty work on D. He did it all.

4. Kevin Love was also very good with 15 points and 15 rebounds. Some of those rebounds came at the offensive end and broke the Sixers' spirit when they thought they might have a chance. Love outclassed young Sixers big men Nerlens Noel and Jahlil Okafor under the basket. His experience in close games really showed. As Cavs radio analyst Jim Chones said, Love was "a man among boys."

5. The brilliance of James and Love overcame tough shooting nights from J.R. Smith (5-of-18) and Kyrie Irving (3-of-15). Tristan Thompson also came through with an underrated 10 points and 10 boards.

6. The reserves struggled mightily — scoring just 11 points and compiling a plus/minus rating of minus-20. Not a huge deal, because everyone has off nights. But again, thank heavens for LeBron James.

7. LeBron on his night/teammates: "They look at me as the leader of this team and I've got to be that way year round. They needed me a lot tonight and I was able to come through."

8. Now, here's something that was shamelessly lifted from Terry Pluto's excellent notes column in the Cleveland Plain Dealer: Dating back to last year right around this time, the Cavs are 41-4 when James, Love and Irving are all in the lineup (regular season). Simply amazing.

9. Something else Pluto mentioned: The Cavs (26-9) were averaging 135 points per 100 possessions in the four games leading up to Sunday. That's best in the NBA. Yet no one really considers the Cavs to be an offensive juggernaut along the lines of the Warriors or some others. But when James, Love and Irving are all playing, the Cavs almost always score at will.

10. For the record, the Cavs are 8-1 this season with their Big Three.

11. Overall, the Cavs have won seven straight. The big Texas swing begins Tuesday in Dallas. Then it's back home Monday for a rematch with the Warriors. Gonna be an intriguing week, for sure.

JANUARY 13

Not perfect, but Cavs win anyway

Random dribbles on the Cavaliers' thrilling 110-107 overtime win over the host Mavericks on Tuesday.

1. LeBron James found himself staring at a wide-open 14-foot jump shot at the elbow. So naturally he passed. To Kyrie Irving. Who was standing about 30 feet from the basket. With the shot clock winding down. With the game in the balance.

2. So Kyrie got the ball. He had one option: Shoot. He did. Cavs win. It really seemed to happen just like that. It really seemed to be over that quickly. Impressive, considering the Cavs didn't exactly appear to have much of a chance for a large part of the night.

3. The Mavericks jumped to a 10-0 lead. They increased it to 23-7. They were playing at home. With Dirk Nowitzki, Chandler Parsons and several others heating it up. They're undoubtedly a good team.

4. Read: The Cavs had every reason to fold. No one would've blamed them if this just wasn't their night. They had already won seven straight. They were already 3-0 on a six-game road trip. And they have another biggie Thursday with a visit to the Spurs. So losing to the Mavs wouldn't have been a letdown. It would've mostly been understandable.

5. But James, Irving and the rest simply weren't going to allow it to happen. This isn't just a talented team. It's one with a great deal of pride. The Cavs believe they're the best in the league. Even Irving has admitted they think about making "statements." Not just to that night's opponent, not just to the rest of the NBA … but to themselves.

6. You probably already know the details. You know about Irving's huge shot with 13 seconds left in OT, James mammoth slam over Devin Harris in the final moments of regulation, Matthew Dellavedova's 3-pointer, then steal off the ensuing inbounds, then 3-pointer.

7. We talk about James, Irving and Kevin Love all the time – and the Cavs' Big Three warrants being at the center of the conversation. But you'd better believe the likes of Delly, J.R. Smith, Tristan Thompson, Iman Shumpert and Timofey Mozgov (yes, Mozgov) are responsible for all this success, too.

8. Early on, neither Irving nor Love could get a thing going. They looked out of sorts and the Cavs suffered because of it. But they didn't mail it in. They never said, "Well, it's just one of those nights." They never thought anything but that they could still somehow win.

9. Love on the evening: "We keep shooting. We always say it only takes one good quarter. Tonight it was overtime."

10. Love also pointed out how "different guys made huge plays." It's true, as Shumpert made the strip of the night on Nowitzki. Shumpert made another important one on Mavs guard Deron Williams. This really was a team effort in the truest sense.

11. And let's not forget Cavs coach David Blatt. A big reason for the players' continued belief is because of their leader — and the way he manages the game, how he throws out different combinations until the right one works. It's never been clearer that Blatt has the trust and support of his team.

12. James finished with 27 points, 10 rebounds and seven assists. Irving

finished with 22 points and nine assists. Love went for 15 points and 11 boards. Dellavedova scored 12, and Shumpert, Smith and Mozgov had 10 apiece.

13. Kyrie on the night: "That's not the team that we want to be (in the first half), but we were still in the game. Talent kept us around for that long, but we locked in in the second half and matched up really well when they went small ball. For us, it's just a luxury having that ability."

14. So make it eight straight wins for the Cavs (27-9) with only two to go in Texas. They are winning in multiple ways — by being flashy, by being scrappy, by taking large leads and never looking back, and by falling behind and making up for it later. It all adds up to a team Cleveland can really get behind. And hey, we're not even at the midpoint of the season yet.

JANUARY 15

Still time for Cavs to conquer league's elite

Random dribbles on the visiting Cavaliers' tough 99-95 loss to the Spurs on Thursday.

1. Can't complain too loudly about this one. The Cavaliers again gave themselves a chance to win on the road against an excellent team. They're still 4-1 on the longest trip of the season, with one to go.

2. I would've written the same thing if the Cavs had won — don't get too excited. It's January. Like I said after the loss at the Warriors, the Spurs still have to come to Cleveland. Like I also said about the Warriors, I'll be a little more concerned if the Cavs lose to the Spurs at home.

3. By the way, both of those home games (vs. the Spurs and Warriors) take place in the next 15 days.

4. This isn't to downplay some of the things the Cavs did wrong. When April, May and June roll around, it can't be: "Well, we kept it close." But as you know, it's a long way before we're wearing t-shirts and shorts in Northeast Ohio again. So yes, it's important to maintain some perspective.

5. Coach David Blatt said the biggest difference was the Cavs stopped moving the ball in the fourth quarter, when the Spurs really tightened their defense. I'd have to agree with that one. It happens too much, too. When

things get close, they suddenly stop doing the things that worked and gave themselves a chance to win. Instead, they sometimes resort to one-on-one play or "hero ball."

6. The Cavs did something similar against the Warriors on Christmas Day. The other area of concern is the Cavs were held below 100 in both of those games. I'm not saying they need to score 120 or more (as they did three straight times last week) — but they need to consistently work for better shots against the league's elite.

7. LeBron James scored 22 points and Kyrie Irving went for 16, but neither got much of anything going in the fourth quarter. Also, Kevin Love was held to just 10 points. When each of the Big Three is contained, the Cavs are really gonna need a miracle to win on the road.

8. They almost got one, as Tristan Thompson (18 points, 14 rebounds) kept making himself available, and delivering, near the basket. But overall, the Cavs just didn't get enough from the guys outside of James and Thompson.

9. Still, if I have to split the two-game series with the Warriors and Spurs, I'd rather win the second. That way you stay in the back of their minds should you meet in the Finals. If nothing else, you don't have to listen to the over-the-top narrative all season should you get swept.

10. Then again, a regular-season sweep doesn't really mean much. I hate to bring it up, but the 1988-89 Cavs won all six games vs. the Bulls in the regular season. But in the first round of the playoffs, those same Cavs succumbed to (you guessed it) Michael Jordan and The Shot.

11. Translation: What happens in January rarely carries over to June. Sure, the Cavs want to win these games. And again, they must start staying with the game plan when things get sticky. But they still have plenty of time to fix those minor issues. They're 27-10 and at the end of a long swing away from home. It's hardly a bad loss.

12. Kyrie on if he's concerned about the losses to the Warriors and Spurs: "No. They gotta come to our home."

13. Spurs forward Kawhi Leonard truly does make James work harder than anyone else in the league. I know I'm repeating what a lot of you already know — but it's one of the few things that you read about over and over from the national media that is actually true.

14. Leonard also keeps James busy on defense, and did so again Thursday. After a slow start, Leonard finished with 20 points, 10 rebounds, and one monster putback slam.

15. The Spurs are such a classy organization, with players who don't ever act anything but professional. I once mentioned all this to Spurs coach Gregg Popovich. He said that's not by accident. "We tend to draft guys who have gotten over themselves," he told me.

16. Anyway, as most coaches will tell you, the great thing about the NBA is there's always another game, another chance to get things right. For the Cavs, that comes quickly — as they visit the Rockets to conclude this massive swing Friday.

17. Win, and the Cavs finish their trip at 5-1. Lose, and it's still 4-2. Either way, it's a doggone good trip. They'll think it's a whole lot better if they return home to beat the Warriors on Monday.

18. LeBron may sit out to rest vs. the Rockets. He said he wants to play, but he plans to discuss it with Blatt on Friday morning.

JANUARY 19

Clearly, Cavs have lots of work ahead

CLEVELAND – Random dribbles from the Cavaliers' 132-98 embarrassment of a loss to the Warriors on Monday.

1. The Cavs didn't show up. There's no other way to spin it. And sometimes teams can "show up" against the Warriors and still get drilled. Hopefully, the Cavs learned a little something about themselves in this game. Because that's the only way it has value — you experience it, you hate it, you learn from it, you improve.

2. There were so many things wrong here it's hard to know where to begin. The ball movement was atrocious from the start. The Cavs seemed hesitant to shoot when they did get an open look. They defended like they had no clue Steph Curry and Warriors could make 3-pointers.

3. The Cavs were flat. They were soft. The Warriors came out hungry, playing with the heart of champions. They'd heard the talk about losing two of three — how maybe they were starting to come back to Earth. Instead

of accepting a dry spell, they used this night to return to their dominant ways.

4. I know. This isn't easy to read. It's sure not easy to write. I thought the Cavs would at least put up a fight. I thought they would capitalize on the fact LeBron James was finally joined by a healthy Kevin Love and Kyrie Irving, that they were playing at home, that they wanted to show the Warriors who's really boss. Then the opposite of that happened.

5. Love scored three points and grabbed six rebounds in 21 minutes. Part of that was because the Warriors turned it into 48 minutes of garbage time. But part of it was because Love has not been nearly aggressive enough in these types of games. Whatever is going on with Love, coach David Blatt needs to solve it.

6. LeBron scored 16 on 7-of-16 shooting. He passed for five assists and grabbed five rebounds. This wasn't LeBron's fault — but those are a far cry from his eye-popping numbers of the Finals.

7. Irving was also contained, scoring just eight points on 3-of-11 shooting. The Warriors smothered the Cavs' Big Three, not giving any of them a decent look at the basket. Overall, the Cavs went 7-of-19 on threes. Curry alone went 7-of-12.

8. Nineteen attempts is actually a low number for the Cavs. The Warriors had a lot to do with that. But the Cavs made it easy on them by not moving the ball or playing an inside-out brand of basketball. Instead, it was dribble, dribble, dribble and dribble some more — then hope something goes in. That might work against the 76ers or even Bobcats. It won't work against the league's elite.

9. The Warriors have true stars in Curry, Klay Thompson and Draymond Green, but they still share the ball. They space the floor. They pass, they cut. They find the open man. They are a very skilled team. They defend hard and suffocate opposing offenses. They're ruthless on the boards. They don't rest on their reputations. Even at their worst (which isn't very often), they will play hard, play smart and challenge you.

10. I don't want to be too dire here. I've been covering the NBA for 20 years. Not once has a champion been crowned in January. Or February. Or March. Or April. Or even May. There is plenty of time for the Cavs to find a rhythm and play the right way and beat the league's best — and I do mean gobs of time. But they have work to do. We saw that Monday.

11. Other less talented teams have bounced back from worse. I know it doesn't seem like it's possible, but believe me. I've seen it. But again, the Cavs (28-11) have hit a speed bump. Maybe this will trigger a trade from GM David Griffin. Maybe the Cavs only need more time to get their chemistry right. Maybe Blatt needs to reorganize the rotation. Mostly, it's not a time for panic or doom and gloom, but for a little evaluation.

12. This was one game and I agree with Warriors interim coach Luke Walton, the former Cavalier. Walton said he doesn't expect this loss will much impact the Cavs — especially with a leader like LeBron. "He's not going to let those guys get intimidated at all," Walton said. "I wouldn't imagine that (loss) does anything to them."

13. LeBron, meanwhile, admitted he didn't have any lectures for his teammates after the game. "I'm not a kick-a-man-when-he's-down type of guy," he said. "That's not my motto."

14. Finally, the Cavs will most certainly bounce back from this. They're too talented not to. They visit the Nets on Wednesday, and the Clippers come to town Thursday. Frankly, I wouldn't want to be either of them. Nor are the Cavs this inferior to the Warriors. The good news is they have more than half a regular season (and all the playoffs) to figure it out — and if both teams make it to June, to show the Warriors that they never forgot this day.

JANUARY 21

Everyone involved as Cavs handle business

Random dribbles on the Cavaliers' 91-78 dismantling of the host Nets on Wednesday.

1. Well, that was more like it. The Cavaliers put this away early and easily, and maybe best of all, Kevin Love was majorly involved. Love finished with 17 points and 18 rebounds and wasn't even needed in the fourth quarter.

2. The same was true of LeBron James (17 points), Timofey Mozgov (11) and Kyrie Irving (nine on 4-of-7 shooting, five assists). All that rest for key players was important, as the Cavs play the Clippers at home Thursday.

3. There isn't too terribly much to take away from this game. The Nets

really stink. It seems like decades ago since Kevin Garnett, Paul Pierce, Deron Williams, Brook Lopez and Joe Johnson donned the cover of Sports Illustrated. Jason Kidd was the coach, and the magazine headline asked, "Who wants a piece of them?"

4. These days, the answer is everyone.

5. Only Lopez and Johnson remain. Lopez is still pretty good, as he scored 16 points and pulled down 10 boards. But the over-the-hill Johnson went 1-of-7 for three points.

6. Anyway, back to the Cavs. They're 29-11, which means Thursday's game is the official midway point. My summary of the first half: a). They will drill opponents such as the Nets just on talent alone; b). Now let's see if they really do stick to their commitment to learning from that horrific loss to the Warriors.

7. Prediction: The Cavs will eventually prove they were impacted by that loss. But it will take some time to get everything corrected — should they meet the Warriors again in June. The key is ball movement, overall determination to make the right play, and defense. There's clearly no shortage of talent or depth. No trades are necessary, and none are likely to happen.

8. Cavs coach David Blatt on bouncing back: "It's painful to get knocked down, but it's shameful not to get back up if you get knocked down."

9. And whether or not the Nets are awful (again, they are) the Cavs needed a night when they were never really threatened. This was it, as everyone contributed and got plenty of playing time. Even Mo Williams saw the floor for the first time in eight games. As I've said on recent radio spots, I'm a big proponent of Blatt finding a way to get more out of Mo.

10. Tristan Thompson also came up big with 14 points and 10 boards, and Matthew Dellavedova scored eight off the bench on 3-of-3 shooting. Thompson was 6-of-8 from the floor.

11. Love scored just three points vs. the Warriors. His take on his bounce-back game: "I wasn't the only one — I felt a lot of guys played with more energy and brought it. But there's really only one way you could go from the last game I had."

12. So overall, it was a good night, a night the Cavs can use to build on, to

maybe study some film, focus on what went right and keep putting it into practice. There is, undoubtedly, a very long way yet to go.

JANUARY 22

With eye on past, Cavs evolving

Random dribbles on the Cavaliers' impressive 115-102 win over the visiting Clippers on Thursday.

1. Clearly, LeBron James and the Cavs have recommitted themselves to good ball movement. James scored 22 points vs. the Clippers — but it was his 12 assists that showed James is serious about keeping things flowing.

2. On Thursday, the Cavs snapped their passes, didn't stand around dribbling and didn't settle for a bunch of perimeter shots. They were aggressive at both ends and stayed in attack mode throughout. This was a good team they beat, and for most of the night, you never really felt they were threatened.

3. Yes, the Cavs launched 3-pointers on 28 occasions. But there's a difference between "settling" and taking a long-range jumper when you're running the offense. J.R. Smith (also 22 points) went 6-of-7 on threes, and he looked set, squared up and comfortable on every last attempt.

4. That's when Smith is at his best. I love Smith's freewheeling game and effort, but rarely do good things happen when he takes more than two dribbles. Interestingly, when the ball moves like it did Thursday, Smith always seems to score in the 20s.

5. By the way, the Cavs outscored the Clippers by a whopping 29 points with Smith on the floor.

6. Kyrie Irving (21 points), Kevin Love (18 and 16 rebounds) and Timofey Mozgov (11 points, 5-of-6 shooting) also had strong performances, and again, it's not surprising. James looked for each of them and delivered the ball to their shooting pockets. While he can sometimes be guilty of the ball "sticking" in one spot as the shot clock winds down, he's also the leader when things run smoothly.

7. A simple eye test tells you what the Cavs said in their meeting after Monday's hammer job of a loss to the Warriors. They've decided to space

the floor, share the ball, be assertive, and not take plays off. Now, they can still lose some games even if they do all that. But what matters is they do it consistently, making a habit out of smart and selfless basketball.

8. Overall, the Cavs seem even more determined, even more cohesive than, well, before Monday.

9. This isn't to say the Cavs were a miserable mess before the previous two games. For Pete's sake, they're 30-11 with exactly half a regular season to go. It's true they got swept by the Warriors and didn't beat the Spurs (the next meeting is a week from Saturday) — but guess what all of that means in January? Yep, nothing.

10. Cavs coach David Blatt deserves a lot of credit here, too. He's never influenced by the media or fans, but even he could see that Love simply was not involved enough. Rather than make excuses, or hope it worked itself out, he made it clear that Love's production needed to change. And it's everyone's responsibility to make it happen.

11. So far, it's worked. In the previous two games, Love is averaging a combined 17.5 points and 17 rebounds.

12. Blatt and the Cavs don't like hearing about it, or really talking about it, but that loss to the Warriors could be something that motivates them to prove the critics wrong. It wouldn't be the first time greatness results from adversity. Without a 34-point home loss, who knows? The Cavs might just be floating their way to good wins on talent alone.

13. Basically, it will be interesting to see if it lasts — but right now, it's pretty evident something has lit a fire under these guys and their overall approach to games.

14. Prior to the tipoff, Blatt expressed a bit of annoyance about the negative things being said and written. "I hear a lot of far-reaching conclusions and, personally, I don't like it," he said. "But there's nothing I can do about it because I'm not the one saying or doing those things."

15. Blatt continued after the win: "It's about my team. It's about my guys and I don't like it. I don't like it at all. My guys are out there fighting for the Cavaliers and doing the best job they can in a tough NBA — very tough — especially because this is a team that night after night has a target on its back. They go out there and they fight and they play and they deal with adversity like we've had to deal with all year. We are far from perfect and

we are still not at our best, but it's not for lack of effort."

16. The Clippers entered the night having won 10 of 11. They've been rolling without star forward Blake Griffin, who's not expected back from a torn quad until next week. The backcourt of Chris Paul (30 points) and J.J. Redick (17) has been particularly impressive lately. But while they both went off in spurts Thursday, the Cavs constantly flew around the court, chased down the ball, and generally made life difficult for the opponent.

17. Finally, LeBron on the streak, and of course, the loss to the Warriors: "Who's to say we shook it off? We won two games. We took two or three steps backward Monday and we took a couple steps forward these last couple games, and that's all that matters to me."

5 THE SWITCH

JANUARY 26

Who's to say Cavs were fine as is?

CLEVELAND — Random dribbles on the Cavaliers' decision to fire coach David Blatt on Friday.

1. General manager David Griffin didn't consult any of the players before firing Blatt. Griffin said it, and I believe it. "I'm not taking a poll," he said at Friday's press conference. Know why he didn't ask the players? Easy. He didn't need to.

2. Obviously, Griffin spends a lot of time in the Cavs' locker room. I've been in there enough. And anyone who's so much as stopped by could see the Cavs haven't had much fire (or fun) after games — even after wins. Or as Griffin said, the Cavs have lacked "spirit."

3. Now, nobody expects an 82-game season to be a yearlong pep rally. But for a team that's 30-11, the Cavs have just seemed sort of … there.

4. Everyone associated with the team knows the loss to the Spurs and recent thrashing by the Warriors weren't entirely Blatt's fault. Still, it's the head coach's job to get the most out of his team, to keep his players motivated, to maintain their respect, to make certain the offense is flowing. All of that dwindled in recent weeks, and it was evident, both on and off the court.

5. It's important to note that when Blatt took the job, the Cavs were a different team with different goals. The roster was young with the likes of Kyrie Irving, Tristan Thompson, Andrew Wiggins, Anthony Bennett and Dion Waiters expected to play major roles. Griffin and owner Dan Gilbert were merely hoping Blatt could push the team to a first-round playoff exit.

6. One month later, LeBron James announced he was returning to Cleveland. Then Griffin traded Wiggins and Bennett to the Timberwolves for Kevin Love. Then Waiters was shipped to the Thunder. Then J.R. Smith, Iman Shumpert and Timofey Mozgov came to town.

7. So half a season after Blatt was hired, the Cavs were suddenly a

championship-caliber club — a far cry from when he took the job. But Blatt was still learning the NBA game after decades overseas. Right away, there were gripes from fans and media about Blatt's sometimes-odd decisions and clunky substitution patterns. "And if we all notice it, imagine how the players feel," one prominent sportswriter covering the Finals said to me in June.

8. This season was more of the same. The Cavs seemed to win almost in spite of Blatt's inability to get Love involved in the offense on a regular basis ... his ongoing unpredictable rotation ... his insistence on keeping battle-tested veterans Mo Williams, Anderson Varejao and Richard Jefferson glued to the bench, even when the Cavs clearly could've used their help.

9. While being respectful of Blatt, Varejao politely hinted at his desire for a consistent role. Jefferson and Williams became very unhappy and began to show it. People within the organization and around the league wondered why Williams, in particular, was dismissed so quickly when he started and played well during an eight-game winning streak earlier in the season.

10. James saw and sometimes heard about the frustration from his respected veteran teammates. He's always OK if guys don't play — but only if they get a real chance and aren't productive. Instead, it was almost as if Blatt just couldn't figure out how to use some of the talent at his disposal. That may not have been the case, but it sure did feel like it.

11. Either way, James never cared for Blatt's philosophy or approach. LeBron never demanded Blatt be fired, and LeBron truly was as surprised as anyone by Friday's news. But there's little doubt he's anything less than 100 percent fine with the change to new coach Tyronn Lue. Overall, the locker room is happy as a whole.

12. Understandably, Gilbert was dismayed following the 34-point loss to the Warriors. Still, he struggled and spent some time in thought after Griffin approached and said it was time to fire the coach. "Sometimes the hardest thing to do is also the right thing to do," Gilbert said in a prepared statement.

13. The Cavs may not be done yet. They have been working on a couple trades, one of which could be fairly noteworthy. Griffin is far from desperate, and the Cavs certainly have the talent to win a title as is — if they can put it all together. Nonetheless, it appears they are exploring what's out there and may even have something stirring.

14. Lue became known for his offensive creativity and overall likability in previous stints as an assistant coach. He relates well to the players without behaving like their best buddy. The current group of Cavs has a great deal of respect for him. In the NBA, that's about 75 percent of it, maybe more. And maybe Lue can do for the Cavs what another former guard-turned-coach, Steve Kerr, did for the Warriors last season.

15. Too much has already been said, written and theorized about how this will all play out, whether LeBron orchestrated it, blah, blah, blah. But the only thing that matters is who is standing alone in June, holding the trophy high above their heads. Bottom line: Griffin felt an immediate coaching change improved the Cavs' shot at that. And to say he's wrong in January or February or March is pure silliness.

JANUARY 26

Lue will need time to solve Cavs

CLEVELAND — Random dribbles on the Cavaliers' decision to fire coach David Blatt on Friday.

1. General manager David Griffin didn't consult any of the players before firing Blatt. Griffin said it, and I believe it. "I'm not taking a poll," he said at Friday's press conference. Know why he didn't ask the players? Easy. He didn't need to.

2. Obviously, Griffin spends a lot of time in the Cavs' locker room. I've been in there enough. And anyone who's so much as stopped by could see the Cavs haven't had much fire (or fun) after games — even after wins. Or as Griffin said, the Cavs have lacked "spirit."

3. Now, nobody expects an 82-game season to be a yearlong pep rally. But for a team that's 30-11, the Cavs have just seemed sort of … there.

4. Everyone associated with the team knows the loss to the Spurs and recent thrashing by the Warriors weren't entirely Blatt's fault. Still, it's the head coach's job to get the most out of his team, to keep his players motivated, to maintain their respect, to make certain the offense is flowing. All of that dwindled in recent weeks, and it was evident, both on and off the court.

5. It is important to note that when Blatt took the job, the Cavs were a different team with different goals. The roster was young with the likes of Kyrie Irving, Tristan Thompson, Andrew Wiggins, Anthony Bennett and Dion Waiters expected to play major roles. Griffin and owner Dan Gilbert were merely hoping Blatt could push the team to a first-round playoff exit.

6. One month later, LeBron James announced he was returning to Cleveland. Then Griffin traded Wiggins and Bennett to the Timberwolves for Kevin Love. Then Waiters was shipped to the Thunder. Then J.R. Smith, Iman Shumpert and Timofey Mozgov came to town.

7. So half a season after Blatt was hired, the Cavs were suddenly a championship-caliber club — a far cry from when he took the job. But Blatt was still learning the NBA game after decades overseas. Right away, there were gripes from fans and media about Blatt's sometimes-odd decisions and clunky substitution patterns. "And if we all notice it, imagine how the players feel," one prominent sportswriter covering the Finals said to me in June.

8. This season was more of the same. The Cavs seemed to win almost in spite of Blatt's inability to get Love involved in the offense on a regular basis ... his ongoing unpredictable rotation ... his insistence on keeping battle-tested veterans Mo Williams, Anderson Varejao and Richard Jefferson glued to the bench, even when the Cavs clearly could've used their help.

9. While being respectful of Blatt, Varejao politely hinted at his desire for a consistent role. Jefferson and Williams became very unhappy and began to show it. People within the organization and around the league wondered why Williams, in particular, was dismissed so quickly when he started and played well during an eight-game winning streak earlier in the season.

10. James saw and sometimes heard about the frustration from his respected veteran teammates. He's always OK if guys don't play — but only if they get a real chance and aren't productive. Instead, it was almost as if Blatt just couldn't figure out how to use some of the talent at his disposal. That may not have been the case, but it sure did feel like it.

11. Either way, James never cared for Blatt's philosophy or approach. LeBron never demanded Blatt be fired, and LeBron truly was as surprised as anyone by Friday's news. But there's little doubt he's anything less than 100 percent fine with the change to new coach Tyronn Lue. Overall, the locker room is happy as a whole.

11. Understandably, Gilbert was dismayed following the 34-point loss to the Warriors. Still, he struggled and spent some time in thought after Griffin approached and said it was time to fire the coach. "Sometimes the hardest thing to do is also the right thing to do," Gilbert said in a prepared statement.

12. The Cavs may not be done yet. They have been working on a couple trades, one of which could be fairly noteworthy. Griffin is far from desperate, and the Cavs certainly have the talent to win a title as is — if they can put it all together. Nonetheless, it appears they are exploring what's out there and may even have something stirring.

13. Lue became known for his offensive creativity and overall likability in previous stints as an assistant coach. He relates well to the players without behaving like their best buddy. The current group of Cavs has a great deal of respect for him. In the NBA, that's about 75 percent of it, maybe more. And maybe Lue can do for the Cavs what another former guard-turned-coach, Steve Kerr, did for the Warriors last season.

14. Too much has already been said, written and theorized about how this will all play out, whether LeBron orchestrated it, blah, blah, blah. But the only thing that matters is who is standing alone in June, holding the trophy high above their heads. Bottom line: Griffin felt an immediate coaching change improved the Cavs' shot at that. And to say he's wrong in January or February or March is pure silliness.

JANUARY 26

Cavs moving, and Love staying

CLEVELAND – Random dribbles from the Cavaliers' 114-107 win over the visiting Timberwolves on Monday.

1. It wasn't the most awesome performance, but forgive the Cavs for maybe treating this game like a scrimmage. They needed a win, they needed the practice, and Andrew Wiggins and the Wolves always give the Cavs their very best. And the Cavs always come out on top, anyway.

2. It was also Tyronn Lue's first victory as an NBA coach. Sometimes, that's the hardest part. Especially when you consider Lue is trying to get the Cavs to play at a faster pace.

3. At times, it looked fantastic. At other times, it was understandably sloppy. The Cavs haven't had much of an opportunity to practice under Lue. As Kyrie Irving said afterward: "There's a lot going on. My mind is going a thousand miles per hour right now."

4. Irving was the epitome of the spread-the-wealth and move-the-ball-quickly philosophy. Like the entire team, he played exceptionally well in spurts, compiling 17 points and a season-high nine rebounds. But he also finished just 7-of-18 shooting and committed four turnovers.

5. Meanwhile, LeBron James went for 25 points on a sizzling 11-of-15 from the floor. He also passed for nine assists. But again, the faster pace sometimes looked forced — with James handing out five turnovers.

6. But this is just the start of a style the Cavs (31-12) hope to master by, oh, April. There is plenty of time to get it right. It helps if they can win a few games and give themselves some separation in the Eastern Conference in the process. On Monday, that's what they did.

7. Lue pointed out that pushing the tempo doesn't mean rushing shots or forcing passes. "We gotta play fast, but not make turnovers," he said.

8. In time, that should happen. And based on Monday's second experiment under Lue, it should be lots of fun when it does.

9. While a lot of Cavs seem to be trying to find their way in the new scheme, Matthew Dellavedova tends to play this way all the time. He was magnificent all around Monday — scoring 18 points and passing for seven assists on Australia Day. "He backed up his day," James said of Delly.

10. Dellavedova on the tempo: "If we move the ball and move bodies ... everyone is going to enjoy playing this style."

11. And man, this sure seems to open up things for Tristan Thompson (19 points, 12 boards) near the basket. He got a few quick dunks and drew some fouls as a result of the whipped passes that came his way. Of course, Thompson also continued to chase every rebound like it was a brick of gold. His determination is perhaps the most underrated aspect of this team.

12. Kevin Love was active but finished with just 11 points and six rebounds. Lue admittedly is still trying to get the power forward going. Love also needs to get himself going by shooting the ball better from the

perimeter. He was just 1-of-7 on 3-pointers.

13. Lue on Love: "I just want Kevin to get comfortable. I know he was comfortable in Minnesota playing on the elbows. That's kind of his niche. So we want to get him back to his comfort zone. I know it's been tough these last couple of games because we're trying to play with pace. Guys are getting tired, which kind of messes with the rotation. Kevin was great. He was fine."

14. Love has been the subject of lots of trade rumors in recent weeks — and hey, what else is new? It seems like Love just can't get a break when it comes to having his name thrown about by the Internet rumormonger-types. But Cavs GM David Griffin shot it all down when he told ESPN: "We've never once put together an offer involving Kevin, nor have we taken a call on an offer for Kevin."

15. Good. The Cavs don't need any more Earth-shattering moves. Make what is here work. We all know it can. We saw it during the second half of last season, when they finished the regular season in a flurry. And if they get back to that level, yes, they can win a title. So let's wait and see. This is January, not May.

16. As for Wiggins, this was probably his worst game statistically against the Cavs. Perhaps it's because he didn't shoot every time he touched it. That's what he did in previous games vs. the Cavs — clearly in some sort of act of revenge for their decision to trade him. This time, he looked more interested in playing a complete game.

17. Also, Lue put defensive ace Iman Shumpert on Wiggins for much of the night. Not surprisingly, things were considerably more difficult for the Wolves' second-year swingman.

18. Wolves rookie center Karl-Anthony Towns (26 points, 11 rebounds) was once again brilliant. This young team will be really good if it ever decides to consistently make him the first option — and quits settling for jumpers so much.

19. Anyway, back to the Cavs. They still have three games this week, including a back-to-back Friday (at Pistons) and Saturday (home vs. Spurs). Four games in six days at a faster pace? It's safe to say this will help the Cavs get in the type of condition their new coach seeks.

JANUARY 28

Cavs show what may be ahead in rout

CLEVELAND — Random dribbles from the Cavaliers' 115-93 pummeling of the visiting Suns on Wednesday.

1. The Cavs needed another game against a vastly inferior opponent, mostly to get a better handle on Tyronn Lue's new approach. They got such an opponent, and they delivered. This particular game really was that simple. It was mostly a practice — and a chance for the Cavs to see they're still explosive when all goes well.

2. The next two games offer much better tests. The Cavs (32-12) visit the Pistons on Friday, then return home to face the Spurs the next night. That's a back-to-back against two teams the Cavs have already lost to on the road.

3. The Pistons manhandled the Warriors last week, and when it comes to the Spurs — well, we all know how the Cavs have fared against some of the league's elite.

4. Nonetheless, I wouldn't put too much into the weekend. If the Cavs can get one of the two, they'll be pretty happy. If they win both, it will show they're picking up steam sooner than even they expected. If they lose both, let's just get it out of the way right now — it's not the end of the world.

5. Lue is admittedly still working on the rotation, and the players are admittedly still figuring out how to play quicker, while playing even smarter. Nor are the Cavs in the type of shape Lue wants for the playoffs in April. Thankfully, the playoffs are still about 11 weeks away, as we're barely past the halfway point of the regular season.

6. Highlights from this game? Start with Kevin Love, who scored 21 points and grabbed 11 rebounds in just 27 minutes. LeBron James also scored 21 points, and did it on 7-of-8 shooting. Yes, LeBron scored that many on just eight shots. He was only needed for the first three quarters.

7. James also passed for nine assists for the third straight game. He's compiled that number in all three games since Lue replaced David Blatt. It's not a coincidence.

8. J.R. Smith added 18 points on 7-of-11 from the floor. Richard Jefferson went 4-of-4 for 14. Overall, the Cavs made 45 shots on 34 assisted baskets.

9. Again, the Suns (14-33) are in a horrible spot. They weren't that good to begin with, and now they are missing their injured starting backcourt of Eric Bledsoe and Brandon Knight. Former Cavs forward Jon Leuer is one of their better players, and he's out, too. And their best player, forward Markieff Morris, seems to want traded and the Suns may soon oblige. They're a mess.

10. That's not the Cavs' problem, though. They're still finding their way under Lue, as they showed as slogging their way to a 55-50 halftime lead. But then they finally turned up the defense, started to push the pace and feel good about themselves — lousy opponent or not.

11. One of the most memorable moments came on fast break when Smith raced down the floor and tossed the ball off the backboard to a trailing James. Monster dunk, crowd goes wild, and hey, the Cavs are having fun again.

12. Lue on the night: "Guys (are) getting a chance to get out and run, getting layups. J.R. Smith got a couple layups, dunks. LeBron got a couple dunks. I think the way we want to play is fun. Everybody gets involved."

13. Lue clinched the Eastern Conference All-Star coaching spot with the win — the Cavs assuring themselves of the best record through the end of the month. Love had some fun with it, telling reporters: "He's won 66 percent of his games so far, right?"

14. Lue on coaching the All-Stars: "It's a tribute to coach Blatt and the players and the hard work the assistant coaches put in to get us to this point. I know my coaches are excited, and I know it's going to be a surreal moment."

15. Kyrie Irving only had eight points, but took just eight shots in 22 minutes. He clearly is still learning what Lue expects — and has admitted as much. But the Cavs are gonna need him near his best this weekend, that's for sure.

JANUARY 30

Now that is what Cavs' Lue wants

Random dribbles on the visiting Cavaliers' impressive 114-106 over the Pistons on Friday.

1. Once the Cavs get a handle on Tyronn Lue's new system, they should be pretty good. As in, great. That's what we learned from this one. The Cavaliers defended, the ball moved, and Kevin Love (29 points, 5-of-7 on 3-pointers) made shots.

2. Kyrie Irving (28 points, 11-of-19 shooting) also looked a lot closer to what we've come to expect. That's good news, as Irving has struggled a bit lately — at least, struggled for him. But against the Pistons, he played perhaps his best defense of the season and did his thing offensively.

3. LeBron James is usually the star of the Cavs' Big Three, and while he didn't score as many points as Love or Irving, he made sure to facilitate. James scored 20 points and grabbed nine rebounds. Also, in each of Lue's first three games, LeBron passed for nine assists. Against the Pistons, he had eight.

4. So in Lue's four games since taking over for David Blatt, the Cavs are 3-1 and James is averaging 8.8 assists. Read: LeBron is truly leading by example when it comes to the Cavs' motto of playing with pace and space.

5. LeBron on the night: "We always talk about, it starts and ends with the 'Big Three,' and those two guys (Love and Irving) got it done. I filled in, did what I needed to do to help us win."

6. You also had to really like the play the Cavs got from the center position vs. the Pistons monster in the middle, Andre Drummond. Cavs starter Tristan Thompson hustled his way to 11 points and 14 rebounds, and Timofey Mozgov came off the bench for 12 points and eight boards. Mozgov looks like a new man under Lue.

7. So the Cavs centers combined for 25 points and 22 rebounds. Drummond finished with 20 and eight. The Cavs will take it.

8. Again, I also thought Irving did his best job defensively since returning from knee surgery. Irving played a large role in harassing talented Pistons point guard Reggie Jackson, who went 6-of-16 shooting, including 0-of-3

on threes.

9. This isn't to say the Cavs (33-12) played the prefect game. But it was clearly their best night under Lue. If they can consistently perform with this type of efficiency, no one will continue to say they're merely the best team in the East.

10. The Pistons (25-22) are much-improved from last season. They seem to have a firm grasp of coach Stan Van Gundy's European brand of basketball. They hammered the mighty Warriors, and the Pistons' style focuses on strong ball movement, good spacing and quality perimeter shooting — a style the Cavs hope to emulate. But the Pistons looked overwhelmed on this night, as the Cavs kept the pressure on (at both ends) for all 48 minutes.

11. Van Gundy wasn't ashamed to give the Cavs credit. "They played really, really well," he said. "So, it's not all on us. I mean, they were terrific."

12. A bigger test takes place Saturday. That's when the Spurs come to town. It will be the second night of a back-to-back for the Cavs. If they give the type of effort they gave Friday, and bury those open jumpers again, they'll win. Basically, what they did Friday, in terms of determination and pace, needs to become a habit.

FEBRUARY 4

When ball stops, so do the Cavs

Random dribbles on the Cavaliers' disheartening 106-97 loss to the host Hornets on Wednesday.

1. LeBron James and Kyrie Irving are the men with the ball in their hands for the Cavaliers. So when the offense isn't running like it should, guess who's to blame?

2. It's true that without James and Irving, the Cavs would never have a chance. They are the biggest reasons why, even after Wednesday's loss, the Cavs are an impressive 35-13. Never forget that about this marathon of an NBA season — the only thing that counts is your record.

3. But the Cavs want to win a championship. In the last two games (one win, one loss) they haven't exactly played championship basketball.

4. I'm not saying the Cavs have no shot at a title. I believe they do. I believe this is one lousy game in February. I believe they have four months to get things figured out. You don't need to be 50-4 or whatever in February. But you do need to pull it together and start displaying good habits on a regular basis.

5. Back to James and Irving. Coach Tyronn Lue wants an offense that flows. He wants the ball to move — quickly. That means making a pass, moving, and hey, if things work out, getting the ball back for a good shot.

6. But Irving dribbles too much. James can sometimes do it, too. If you can't get something going in four or five dribbles, give it up. Go set a screen. Roll to the basket. Quit standing around. Quit trying to go one-on-one. Quit making life difficult for yourself. And guess what? You don't have to shoot it every time you're open. Sometimes, there's a better shot out there. This isn't brain surgery. Basketball is a game of constant motion. Teams that adhere to such a philosophy are usually the ones that win.

7. Now, there are times when Irving (26 points) and James (23) do need to just take over. That's why you have stars — so when all else fails, you can still have hope. Kyrie and LeBron offer that. Sometimes, the Cavs need it. But it's important for the stars to realize that sometimes, it takes a team. The Cavs' best players must show they really believe that, and they must start doing it regularly.

8. Kevin Love (12 points, 12 rebounds) took three shots in the second half. How does that ever happen? And what's the point of having a Big Three if all three of them don't function as a unit? Love needs the ball. He needs it in his spots. He can't just be stationed far from the hoop where he watches Irving dribble. That doesn't do anyone any good.

9. Again, this isn't intended to bash anyone or make it sound like the season is lost. Far from it. Every team in the NBA loses games it should win. This was unquestionably one of those games, as the Hornets (24-25) were without Kemba Walker and Al Jefferson. But no issue here with a loss. It's how the Cavs lost that should aggravate them.

10. The defense wasn't much better, as Cavs centers Tristan Thompson and Timofey Mozgov were pushed around on both ends. James, Irving and Mo Williams (filling in for the injured Matthew Dellavedova) served up too many good looks from the outside. About the only person who really got after it on D was J.R. Smith. Even Iman Shumpert struggled.

11. Translation: Gentlemen, this is the NBA. Because of your star power, you're a targeted team. You need to show up against everyone.

12. The third quarters of the previous two games have also been a miserable mess. The Cavs came out of the locker room flat-footed, stopped moving the ball, and watched as the opponent gobbled up countless rebounds. The good news is, they're talented enough to make all that stop. But it's not gonna just happen. They have to make it happen.

13. LeBron on that very subject: "We're (terrible) in the third quarter right now. We need to figure it out. I don't know what it is. I know Coach and the coaching staff are trying to pinpoint what the case may be. We've got to figure that out."

14. Finally, LeBron has really continued to struggle from the perimeter. It feels like he hasn't made a 3-pointer in a month. He is working way too hard for his points — and it's because he can't hit a jumper. That is something else he needs to get figured out before the playoffs.

15. Since I'm often asked about why James is missing so much, I'll give it my best shot. I'm no shot doctor. But again, it typically comes down to the basics. Stop fading away. Square up. Eyes on the rim. Elbow in. Follow through. Folks in the know have said James works on his shot so much that he may have worked himself right into some bad habits. But bottom line: When things aren't working, stick with the fundamentals. James and the Cavs could use a reminder like that after a loss like this.

FEBRUARY 6

LeBron, Cavs need to get it together

Random dribbles on the Cavaliers' stunner of a 104-103 loss to the visiting Celtics on Friday.

1. The Cavaliers are 35-14. That's about the last positive thing you will read here.

2. The Cavs have looked bad for the better part of their last two games — three if you count the overtime win at Indiana that they almost gave away. I'm agitated. The fans are outraged, and I don't blame them. Now all we need is for the Cavs to get mad and start showing some real passion, too.

3. This isn't to say the Cavs have failed to play hard. They do, but not enough. What they especially haven't done lately is play smart and maintain their focus. They don't stick with what's working — and for the 237th time, that's moving the basketball. Seriously, when they move the ball, they're a completely different team. They're a winning team. They may even be a championship team.

4. They also miss too many free throws. Prior to the game-winning 3-pointer from Celtics guard Avery Bradley, the Cavs went 21-of-35 on free throws. You took THIRTY-FIVE foul shots! You missed 14. You lost by one. Make eight more and this isn't even a game. Make THREE more and you still win!

5. Again, that's just a lack of focus at this level. That's not concentrating on the little things — and the little things are typically the difference in the game. Heroic plays and awesome dunks are rarely the difference. They just get you on the highlight shows.

6. So the Cavaliers need to decide: Do they want to make the highlight shows, or do they want a championship? Do they want to pretend they're auditioning for the world's greatest one-on-one tournament — or do they want to play team basketball and give themselves a chance to make Cleveland history? I wish I had a clear-cut answer. Right now, sorry, but I can't tell.

7. It is on LeBron James to take charge. You've changed coaches. You've helped management land some players, many of whom are players you supposedly trust. You are the only star on the team with championship rings. You need to get mad. You need to lead by example. You need to take control of the locker room. You need to understand the following truth: A team only goes as far as its brightest star takes it.

8. James finished with 30 points, seven rebounds and four assists. Those are winning numbers, for sure. But winning numbers aren't enough. Again, you're the leader. Demand more from yourself. Demand more from your teammates. Play angry. And for Pete's sake, figure out what's wrong with your jumper. If not for anyone else, at least for yourself. LeBron has to work way too hard for his points these days. And it's because he can't shoot.

9. James finished 9-of-23 from the floor, including 0-of-5 on 3-pointers. He again struggled from the line (12-of-17). This isn't to say LeBron has failed

to put in the work. He sometimes maybe works himself into a corner, though. Remember, he always shot the ball very well from the perimeter until his "second coming" to Cleveland.

10. Since then, things seem dicey (at best) anytime James shoots from beyond 15 feet. He has to recognize it and repair it for the Cavs to have a real chance at a championship. He's made them before. He can do it again.

11. I'm calling out James here because he's called himself "the best player in the world." He's really not anymore. He's certainly still up there — but all of that is beside the point anyway. What James' need to be is the best leader in the world. What James' team needs is a swift kick in the butt. And what James needs to do is become the man who gives it to them.

12. James is 31 years old. He hasn't won a championship since the age of 28. Again, that's not meant to be cruel or do anything other than state a fact. And he is a man who is very concerned with his legacy.

13. Even in these days of players cashing in on major endorsements before their first playoff victory, legacies are still measured in rings. LeBron has two. It's no one's fault but his own now if he doesn't get a third. New coach. Many of the teammates you wanted. Good overall health. James needs to realize all this, he needs to take a stand, and he needs to insist the Cavaliers play the right way and at a championship level — then go out there and continuously show them how to do it.

14. Kevin Love left with a deep thigh bruise. Until then, he had scored just 10 points on 4-of-10 shooting. He managed that in 22 clunky minutes. There are too many nights where Love looks uncomfortable out there. Former coach David Blatt was partly to blame for that before, and current coach Tyronn Lue is partly to blame for it now. It's also on Love. Too many nights, he's too content to just stand around and wait for the ball. For a guy who rebounds as much as he does, overall, he's been too soft lately.

15. Love isn't alone. This is an entire team that needs to toughen up and start behaving like champions. Nobody is going to hand you the game because you've made a lot of commercials. In fact, they're gonna come after you even harder. You would think the Cavaliers would know that by now.

16. The Celtics (30-22) play extremely hard under wily coach Brad Stevens. They trailed by 15 points in the first half, yet never lost focus. They trailed by four with 7 seconds left! Isaiah Thomas is their lone All-Star, and he's 5-foot-nothing. He's the former No. 60 overall pick in the draft. That means

he was selected with the very last pick. But Thomas is a real gamer. He plays with a chip on his shoulder. He dares you to try to beat him. He plays like you want the Cavs to play.

17. The Celtics don't compare to the Cavs when it comes to raw talent. It's not even close. But they believe in the system. They trust their teammates. They get after it defensively. They make their free throws. They never think they're out of it. They stick with what has worked for them — even if it stops working for a stretch. They man up, earn their paychecks, and realize that no one in this league is gonna give you an inch. So they go out and they take it from you.

18. Meanwhile, Kyrie Irving (19 points) doesn't look the same. And I write that after one of his better all-around games of the season. Maybe he's not all the way back from the knee injury. But all the way back or not, he's out there. From what I can see, Irving tends to hijack the offense by trying to take over. That's OK once in a while. Sometimes that's the best option. I trust Irving with the ball in his hands late in games. At least he makes his free throws. But there's a difference between taking over and forcing the issue. Irving needs to start showing he understands that difference.

19. Frankly, J.R. Smith (20 points) has been mostly great. He's committed a few silly fouls and taken some ill-advised shots, but at least he's out there trying to make something happen. Smith really wants to win. You can see it in his eyes. He's stepped up defensively this season. Still, Smith is supposed to be your fourth or fifth option. It's OK if he's Nos. 1 or 2 on some nights – but those long Smith dagger shots often seem to bail out the Cavs, as opposed to coming within the flow of the offense. At least, that was the case Friday.

20. OK, I've angrily rambled on long enough. This team, as is, has championship potential. And the Cavs are certainly capable of rattling off another seven or eight straight wins and making us forget all this. But they can't just keep saying they want to "play with pace." They can't just keep saying they want to win a title. They have go out, put their words into action, start getting serious, start getting focused and start playing to their potential. And it all begins and ends with their leader. There is, after all, nowhere else left to turn.

FEBRUARY 7

For Cavs, win can serve as lesson

CLEVELAND – Random dribbles from the Cavaliers' 99-84 win over the visiting Pelicans on Saturday.

1. This still wasn't exactly what the Cavs were looking for offensively, but it's hard to find fault with a 15-point victory. So no complaints.

2. The Cavs (36-14) won by 15 points on the second night of a back-to-back. They never trailed after the first few moments. Yes, it got sloppy at times — but you never felt the Pelicans actually had a real chance to win. Perhaps the best thing for the Cavs was they played with a lot more energy and focus for the majority of the night.

3. Kyrie Irving gave a strong showing with a game-high 29 points on 11-of-21 shooting. LeBron James went for 27 on 11-of-20, and passed for eight assists. The Cavs are 5-1 when James passes for seven or more assists under coach Tyronn Lue. So when LeBron moves the ball, good things happen.

4. Kevin Love was out with a thigh bruise, so Timofey Mozgov started at center and Tristan Thompson switched to power forward. Unlike Love, Thompson isn't going to stretch an opposing defense by being a threat from the perimeter. In fact, Thompson took just four shots — and missed all. But he was still outstanding under the basket, pulling down 15 rebounds and just generally creating havoc.

5. Then there's J.R. Smith. He continued to be aggressive at both ends, scoring 20 points and staying active on defense. Basically, Smith just needs to keep playing with this level of intensity.

6. Anderson Varejao came off the bench for 27 valuable minutes, grabbing 10 rebounds and exhibiting his typical wild ways. "He was very important," Lue said, before adding that one of Varejao's greatest contributions was "just being a pest."

7. And since I always rip the Cavs for missing free throws, it's only fair I mention this: They finished 7-of-7 from the line vs. the Pelicans. On the downside, they shot 35 in Friday's loss to the Celtics ... but just seven Saturday. Only Irving (4-of-4) and James (3-of-3) even went to the line. Statistically, it was kind of a weird night all the way around.

8. Perhaps that's why Lue wasn't all giddy after the game. He said the Cavs still run a "random" offense after an opponent's made basket, that they must start doing a better job of sticking with the game plan. "We need to get better," he said. "A lot better."

9. The Cavs have a great chance to put together another winning streak. If they don't, something's awry. They get the Kings at home Monday — and the Kings are again in shambles, with coach George Karl reportedly on the hot seat. After that it's the Lakers, who are playing for little more than the No. 1 overall draft pick. Old friend Byron Scott returns, and from the sound of things, he too will be looking for another coaching gig after the season.

10. The Cavs then get another shot at the Bulls (Feb. 18, after the All-Star break). That one is also at home. The Cavs lost at Chicago in the first game of the season, then at home a couple weeks ago, one day after Lue replaced David Blatt.

11. It was nice to see Pelicans guard Norris Cole score a career-high 26 points on the same day Cleveland State retired his number. Cole is a good guy who plays hard every night. He is among the top two or three defensive point guards in the league. Cavs fans were mostly happy that Cole's cool day didn't result in a Cavs loss.

12. The Pelicans (18-32) aren't very good, but man, is Anthony Davis (24 points, 11 rebounds) a joy to watch. He may not win league MVP, but a lot of folks would pick him first if they were starting a team today.

13. Both Love and Matthew Dellavedova (hamstring) could return Monday vs. the Kings. Neither injury is believed to be serious. Delly has sat out three straight, and the Cavs miss his defense and energy.

14. Final word from LeBron: "It's ongoing. ... We are still getting there. ... As a former point guard, Coach Lue is continuing to help me."

FEBRUARY 9

It only pays to be a King in Cleveland

Random dribbles on the Cavaliers' 120-100 hammer job of the visiting Kings on Monday.

1. It's hard to put too much into this one, because the Kings are such a mess. They've given up on their coach, and not surprisingly, George Karl is expected to be fired before the weekend because of it.

2. Mostly, the Kings simply do not defend. This is the same team that gave up 74 points to the Celtics on Sunday — in the first half.

3. Karl has made a lot of money, done what he's loved to do and secured his place in NBA (and Cavaliers) lore. But it's still sad to see how the Kings are treating him. The story is out there — so just fire the guy already. Why are you dragging it on when it's being reported by every major outlet? Either deny the reports and offer public support, or let the man go.

4. Kings fans are indebted to owner Vivek Ranadive for keeping their favorite team in Sacramento. Other than that, this organization has become a circus, and it starts at the very top. Ranadive gets too involved and tries to make basketball decisions when, clearly, he doesn't know basketball. He knows business and money. So here's a bit of free advice for some of the ultra-rich guys: Stick with what you know.

5. I'm not saying Karl is the best coach for this franchise. I do think he's a good coach. But I also think his act can get old real fast with the players.

6. And I'm not saying DeMarcus Cousins is the entire problem. The All-Star big man has certainly had his ups and downs, as far as being a team player and always saying the right thing. But he is extremely talented and he's never once indicated he wants out. In fact, he really seems to like being a part of the Kings organization. In some ways, I admire Cousins.

7. But trying to make Cousins the cornerstone isn't working. The Kings should ship him out, start over and create a new culture. And they should do it within the next nine days, before the NBA trade deadline.

8. Then again, that's just my first thought. The other thought is, hey, why not just keep it together and see what transpires? Thirty-one years ago, Karl was a young coach with the Cavs. That team started 2-19 while Karl very

publicly feuded with Cavs star World B. Free. This wasn't casual hints on Instagram or Twitter — this was Karl and Free out-and-out bashing each other in the newspapers on a daily basis.

9. But suddenly and unexpectedly, everything corrected itself. Karl and Free agreed to disagree. The Cavs went on to make the playoffs, and they gave Larry Bird's Celtics all they could handle in the first round. The Celtics eventually advanced, but the final overall score of the series was tied. These Kings, as is, can still make the playoffs. It sounds outlandish, but I've seen crazier things happen with Karl, and it was right here in Cleveland.

10. Anyway, back to today's Cavs. Perhaps the only quote worth noting came from coach Tyronn Lue and his take on the Chinese New Year, celebrated Monday. "I have a great Asian following. ... They think I'm Asian because my last name is 'Lue.'"

11. Other than that, this was little more than a scrimmage. The Cavs (37-14) needed to take care of business, and they did so, quickly. The big story of course was that LeBron James compiled his first triple-double of the season — 21 points, 10 rebounds, 10 assists. That was in just the first three quarters. Unlike some younger stars of some other unnamed teams, James chooses not to play in the fourth quarter of blowouts just so he can rack up bigger stats.

12. Kyrie Irving wasn't too shabby himself, by the way. The Cavs point guard finished with 32 points, 12 assists and just two turnovers in 35 minutes. There was a time when the Kings' Rajon Rondo defended Irving very well. But Rondo was with the Celtics then. He's not been the same since he left. Irving was magnificent.

13. Kyrie wasn't selected for the All-Star Game this weekend and mostly seems relieved. He's repeatedly stated he plans to use the time to gather himself after being forced to play catch-up (he missed the first 24 games), as well as having to deal with the rather unexpected coaching change and change of pace.

14. J.R. Smith gave another fine showing with 22 points. If he keeps it up, the Cavs are going places. Actually, they are anyway.

15. Meanwhile, Kevin Love returned from a one-game absence (thigh bruise) and scored 11 points on just 2-of-10 shooting. Man, I'd really love to see Love get in the swing of things here soon. There are nights he looks like the best power forward in the league. There are others when he's just

sort of ... there. Every night of something in between would suffice.

FEBRUARY 11

Cavs break, then it's time to rise

Random dribbles following the Cavaliers' 120-111 win over the visiting Lakers on Wednesday.

1. This was everything it was supposed to be — a cakewalk, and a nice farewell to Kobe Bryant, as the Lakers legend played his final game at Quicken Loans Arena.

2. It was also the final game before the All-Star break. The Cavs don't play again until Thursday, Feb. 18 at home vs. the Bulls.

3. Kyrie Irving scored 35 points, dominating the befuddled (and typically defenseless) Lakers guards. And my guess is this wasn't just Bryant's final game at The Q as a Laker. My guess is the same will probably be true of Lakers coach Byron Scott. Nice guy who has been stuck in some bad situations — and not exactly made them much better.

4. Anyway, Irving is looking much more nimble as the team heads into the break. He's still dominating the ball a little too much for coach Tyronn Lue's liking — but old habits die hard. Plus, you can't complain too loudly when Irving has scored 30 or more in back-to-back games and the Cavs have won three straight.

5. With 30 regular-season games remaining, the Cavs (38-14) also hold a three-game lead over the Raptors for first place in the East.

6. As is often the case, LeBron James won his battle with Bryant — with James scoring 29 points on 12-of-22 shooting and passing for 11 assists. Kobe scored 17 on 5-of-16 shooting. But nobody claims this is a fair fight these days. Age and injury have caught up with Kobe, as they eventually do us all.

7. Still, you had to admire how Bryant really got after LeBron defensively, particularly in the second half. The Lakers won't make the playoffs this season, but Kobe refuses to play like anything than less than a champion. His body just refuses to give him the same results.

8. Bryant was clearly touched by the love he received from Cavs fans at The Q. "I appreciate the amount of respect the fans gave me here tonight," he said softly.

9. I don't always admire the way fans behave (I'm sure a lot of fans themselves will agree), but Bryant's right. It's rare that an entire crowd conducts itself with so much class. That much was evident just from watching the broadcast.

10. As for the Cavs, I was mostly impressed with how LeBron took it upon himself to move the ball and create for his teammates. I thought this was his best game of the season in terms of passing. He didn't stand around dribbling very often. Instead, he drove to the basket, drew defenders and dumped it off to someone near the hoop.

11. That type of ball movement is one reason Tristan Thompson finished with 15 points on 6-of-6 shooting. Thompson also corralled 13 rebounds. He hasn't necessarily made major strides since last year — but he is a major factor when it comes to how far the Cavs advance.

12. Kevin Love went just 2-of-9 shooting before injuring his surgically-repaired left shoulder late in the second quarter. He never returned, but said it felt fine after the game. He doesn't expect to miss any time.

13. So what's next for the Cavs? Well, after the break last season was when they really turned it on. They will need to do it again. They will need to be even better. They have their eye on a championship, and no less than Bryant said he things they can win it.

14. But the ball needs to move, the Cavs must start defending better, and James needs to lead the way. On the bright side, I've covered LeBron a long time, and I can tell you since his days in Miami, he very obviously turns it up as April and the postseason get closer.

15. It should be an intriguing second half under Lue. Can his message of pace and space get through? Will the Cavs be at their best when it means the most? Last season, they overcame a 19-20 start, some midseason trade rumors and unsubstantiated reports of inner-turmoil. They made it to the Finals when some figured they wouldn't get out of the second round.

16. This year, things have gone much better. Then again, all a lot of people see is how much better things are going for the Warriors and Spurs, too. That's understandable. But keep this in mind: All that matters in this league

is what happens in June. And what happens after the All-Star break will tell us everything we need to know about these Cavs.

6 TRIALS

FEBRUARY 19

Varejao will always be a Cavs hero

CLEVELAND — Anderson Varejao approached me two summers ago at a Cavaliers golf outing.

"Hey, Sam," he said. "Can I get a picture?"

Imagine that. A professional athlete, asking a member of the media for a selfie.

This wasn't because Varejao knows me all that well. It wasn't because I'm some sort of celebrity (far from it), and it wasn't because Varejao thought I'd only write nice things about him or say nice things on TV. And as far as I can tell, it wasn't because he needed a ride home.

It was because that's just Varejao.

He's a kind man, a fun-loving man, a warm man, a man who everyone wants as a friend. Perhaps because it's a role he so willingly plays. He wants to be your friend, too.

Interestingly, this persona was basically the opposite of Varejao during his 12 years on the court for the Cavs. Oh, he wasn't a troublemaker. He was just so, well ... IN YOUR FACE.

The guy has no "off" button. Coaches and teammates referred to him as The Energizer Bunny. Cavs point guard Kyrie Irving once went on and on about how Varejao "will run through a brick wall for you."

To fans, he's forever The Wild Thing — his long curly hair and endless effort making him look like the world's largest dust storm.

Then suddenly, as we sometimes see in the business of basketball, Varejao was gone, shipped off to the Trail Blazers, just another piece in a three-team trade.

It felt heartless, cold, unfair. But that wasn't the intent of Cavs general manager David Griffin, who made the deal. It was actually quite the opposite of Griffin's intent.

Griffin didn't set out to trade Varejao. The GM merely wanted to improve the team. That is the GM's job. Unfortunately, Varejao was the last remaining chip Griffin had to deal.

It was a difficult phone call. In fact, Griffin will tell you that informing Varejao he'd been traded was the hardest basketball call Griffin ever had to make.

But in the end, the Cavs landed Channing Frye, a 6-foot-11 veteran from the Magic who can fill it up from the perimeter and space the floor. On paper, it was a good basketball decision. Frye looks to be a better fit.

That won't make it hurt any less. Not at first, anyway.

The Cavs won Thursday, handling the Bulls in one of their best games of the season. But the locker room was far from joyous afterward. LeBron James, Tristan Thompson and the rest very clearly missed their friend.

ONE LAST SHOT

Varejao may have been the longest-tenured athlete in Cleveland sports before the trade. He's certainly among the most appreciated, maybe loved more than any other.

Of course, the business side of this will continue for Varejao. The Blazers are expected to cut him before he plays a game. They just wanted his contract — then to quickly remove it from the books. For the second time in a day or two, Varejao will hear he's not needed, that he's just "an asset."

Eventually, someone will pick him up. It will likely be another contender. Teams had been trying to pry him away from the Cavs for years.

And why not? Who wouldn't want that hustle, that spirit — that constant irritation of opponents and uncanny ability to bring his own teammates together? Varejao can do both just by walking in the room.

Now, before you ask, NBA rules prohibit Varejao from returning to the Cavs, at least not for one year to the day he was traded. For those of you counting, that's Feb. 18, 2017. It's highly unlikely it happens, even then. Both parties have likely moved on. It's not an emotional parting of ways. It's just business. Good business, but sad business.

But we'll see Varejao again. He'll just be in another uniform. It may even be this season. Some of us may shed a tear. A lot of us will shed a lot, actually.

For now, though, Varejao is just gone. He won't be coming back. And he is truly taking a piece of Cleveland's heart with him.

That's why we have to ask, before you go: Hey, Andy … can we get a picture?

FEBRUARY 22

Cavs display post-break passion

Random dribbles on the Cavaliers' 115-92 dismantling of the host Thunder on Sunday.

1. All that matters is what happens after the All-Star break. I've written that time and again. Right now, in the two games since last weekend, the Cavaliers look at least as good as anyone in the league, probably better.

2. It's one thing to beat a shorthanded Bulls team at home. It's quite another to handle Kevin Durant, Russell Westbrook and the Thunder in their own building.

3. Dating back to before the break, the Cavs have won five straight. And man, they're just hammering people lately. As Joe Gabriele of Cavs.com tweeted, the Cavs have held at least a 20-point lead in each of their previous four games. In the last five games, "no opponent has held a lead after the first quarter," Gabriele wrote.

4. It should be noted the Warriors lost their first game after the break by 32 points. Again, repeat after me: All that matters is what happens after the All-Star break.

5. LeBron James (25 points, 11 assists) has always understood that, and you can just see it on his face and by the way he conducts himself on the court. LeBron is almost always incredible. In these last two games, he's returned to Best Player in the World status. More importantly, he's displaying plenty of energy and making sure the Cavs move the ball.

6. This also was Kevin Love's best game of the season. There's no official stat for that — I'm just going by the eye test. The Cavs needed a huge day from Love. They were playing at a West power, Kyrie Irving left with a stomach issue after nine minutes, and the Cavs were also without Iman Shumpert (shoulder stinger).

7. Love was aggressive, demanded the ball, and seemed to almost laugh as helpless Thunder big man Serge Ibaka helplessly tried to defend. When Love and James play like that, well, all you need is to throw in some steady point guard play from Irving — and no one will beat this team in a seven-game series when it means the most. No one.

8. Of course, all of that is contingent on the Cavs playing this way on a consistent basis. They can't just do it a couple times a week. But I'm starting to think LeBron is really turning it on, Love and Kyrie have plans to join him, and the entire team is starting to grasp new coach Tyronn Lue's offense.

9. It's that last part that should have Cavs fans especially excited. This team has three of the brightest individuals in the game. If they share the ball like Lue wants … well, see point No. 7.

10. Everyone got in on the act Sunday. Tristan Thompson was again brilliant with 14 points and 14 boards. Richard Jefferson and J.R. Smith performed like true veterans, scoring 15 apiece. Timofey Mozgov continued to look like his second-half self of a season ago with 11 points on 5-of-7 shooting. And Matthew Dellavedova passed for seven assists off the bench.

11. I know a lot of Cavs fans are upset with the news that Anderson Varejao signed with the Warriors. You can read my report here. But as much as many Cavs fans dislike the Warriors, they do play basketball the right way. I've covered the NBA for 20 years and I'm not sure I've seen such an unselfish team. The Warriors don't just take the best shot — they take the better-than-best. Varejao is also one of the most selfless players I've covered. So he'll fit in very well there.

12. And that is why Varejao signed with the Warriors. It wasn't to "spite" his former team or city. It was because he believes the Warriors give him the best chance to play and will maximize his skill-set.

13. That said, it's OK for Cavs fans to root against the Warriors and still for Varejao. Or better yet, just root for your own team and check in on Andy.

14. Finally, it appears new acquisition Channing Frye (obtained in the Varejao trade) will be ready to roll Tuesday after he completes his physical and gets moved. The Cavs actually won't practice that day, since they're playing a second game in two nights Monday vs. the Pistons. But despite the delay, there are no known issues when it comes to Frye eventually getting in a Cavs uniform.

FEBRUARY 23

Lack of zip zaps LeBron, Cavs

CLEVELAND — Random dribbles from the Cavaliers' 96-88 defeat to the visiting Pistons on Monday.

1. Too much is often made of these losses, but you don't want to just blow it off, either. The Cavs need to find a way to win games like these — home games against young and hungry teams that are just dying to stick it to LeBron James, Kyrie Irving and Kevin Love.

2. The Cavs (40-15) also want to give themselves some separation in the East playoff race. It won't matter much if they don't land the No. 1 seed. At least, not if they stay healthy. As James said last season, "Just get me in the playoffs." But usually, having more home games than road is a good thing.

3. Speaking of LeBron, he wasn't very LeBron-like. He struggled mightily to the tune of 12 points on 5-of-18 shooting, and led an ugly night of offense with six turnovers. And that outside shot, oh, that outside shot. LeBron was 0-of-4 on 3-pointers.

4. Cavs coach Tyronn Lue on James: "It was one of those games. You know, one of those odd games that you rarely see him play."

5. Now, no one says much about James' jumper when the Cavs win, and they do win quite a bit. But win or lose, it will help the Cavs capture a title if James is a little more consistent from deep. But I've been saying that since he returned to Cleveland. Not much has changed.

6. I sat next to a scout from an opposing team and he basically shrugged off the loss. "The Pistons hammered the Warriors, too," he said. "They do have that potential." One problem with Andre Drummond, Reggie Jackson and the Pistons is they don't often get fired up enough for everyone outside the Cavs and Warriors.

7. The Cavs entered the night having won five straight. The Pistons (28-29) had lost five straight. I rarely know what to expect anymore.

8. Kyrie Irving finished with 30 points, but 21 shots are probably too many. Kevin Love scored 24 and grabbed seven rebounds — carrying a magnificent performance from Sunday's win at the Thunder into this one. But he wasn't nearly as utilized in the second half, and I can't help but

wonder why.

9. The Cavs trailed by 17 points in the second half — then Timofey Mozgov came off the bench and provided a major spark defensively. The Pistons basically stopped driving, as Mozgov stood in the lane and protected the basket.

10. The opposing scout on Mozgov: "Everyone wants to play small because of the Warriors. But you don't need to do that. If you have a guy who can protect the basket, use him. Those guys are rare and they are invaluable."

11. LeBron on what was lacking: "Energy. Didn't like the energy from myself all the way down to everyone else."

12. Tristan Thompson tends to struggle against the much larger Drummond (who doesn't?), and Thompson was way off on this night. He managed just two shots for 0 points with six rebounds – well below his average. I always say that when the ball moves, Tristan is often the Cavs' biggest beneficiary. The fact he got just two shots tells me the ball didn't move.

13. Anyway, no need to panic over this one. The Cavs have a couple things to work on, no doubt. Everyone does. They've got time. Let's just see how it goes. I'd be more worried if they also lost at home Wednesday vs. the Hornets.

FEBRUARY 25

This is why Cavs got that Frye guy

CLEVELAND — Random dribbles from the Cavaliers' fairly easy 114-103 win over the visiting Hornets on Wednesday.

1. Statistically, Channing Frye probably gave the Cavs more than even they expected. He scored 15 points in his first eight minutes — finishing 5-of-9 from the floor, including 4-of-8 on 3-pointers.

2. Remember, this was just his second game as a member of the Cavs. Remember, he hasn't even gone through a real practice with the team.

3. LeBron James has told Frye to shoot the ball every time James passes it to him. "I won't throw it to him unless I know he's got a shot," James said.

4. More James on Frye: "He adds another dynamic to our team that we didn't have."

5. Granted, Frye isn't going to do this every game (at least, that's my guess) — but LeBron put it perfectly. Frye truly does add a lengthy long-range bomber off the bench, acting as another "stretch four" behind Kevin Love. And that truly is something the Cavs didn't have before last week's trade that shipped out Anderson Varejao.

6. Frye isn't a great shot-blocker or known for his defense, but he does get in the way and use his 6-foot-11 frame and long arms to occasionally alter shots. It will be interesting to see him in the game with rim-protecting center Timofey Mozgov on a regular basis.

7. Mostly, Frye gives the Cavs a versatile and experienced big man who can play on the perimeter. He has been at his best with other really good players around him. Nights like Wednesday make it easy to believe he could prove to be a very underrated pickup when it matters most.

8. After the game, Frye briefly addressed the crowd during an interview with the in-arena host. Frye's best line: "I guess I'm doing alright."

9. Cavs coach Tyronn Lue said Frye went to the practice facility Tuesday and went over some plays with the coaching staff. The message to Frye has been simple. "Get to your spots and let Kyrie, LeBron and Delly hit you," Lue said. "He was able to get some open shots."

10. James and Kyrie Irving (23 points apiece) played a balanced overall game and rarely forced a thing. James took 18 shots in Monday's loss to the Pistons and scored just 12 points. He took just 13 shots vs. the Hornets for his 23.

11. J.R. Smith (16 points) also had a nice night, including one crazy three where he sort of dribbled slowly with his back to the basket ... appeared to almost lose the dribble ... then spun around and buried the shot. That, folks, is the beauty of J.R.

12. Yes, Love struggled, scoring eight points and grabbing just two rebounds. But it's hard to complain too much. Up until this one, Love had been magnificent since the All-Star break and the Cavs won.

13. Not surprisingly, Matthew Dellavedova was also pretty efficient, scoring

10 points and passing for seven assists in 26 minutes. Meanwhile, Tristan Thompson had a few fantastic putbacks and grabbed 10 boards.

14. Mostly, the Cavaliers played with pace and took care of the ball. During one 20-minute stretch that started in the second quarter, they didn't commit a single turnover. And during that stretch, their lead expanded from 11 points to 22.

15. For those wondering, Anderson Varejao made his Warriors debut Wednesday in a 118-112 win over the Heat. Varejao scored one point and grabbed three rebounds in 10 minutes. "It's great to be part of a winning organization, a great organization, one that's very well coached and with great players," he said.

16. In case you missed it, here is a video assessment from USA Today's Jeff Zillgitt on Varejao.

17. Finally, let's see how the Cavs (41-15) fair in Friday's biggie at Toronto. The Raptors (38-18) have won three straight, and are just three games behind the Cavs for the top spot in the Eastern Conference.

FEBRUARY 27

Time for Cavs to finish these jobs

Random dribbles on the Cavaliers' toughie of a 99-97 loss to the host Raptors on Friday.

1. No one who roots for the Cavs likes how this one went down — but sorry, I'm still not all that worried about the Raptors if I'm the Cavs. The Cavs fell apart here, for sure. But I don't see any major signs that the Raptors could beat them in a seven-game series.

2. Again, this isn't intended to downplay several of the Cavs' late-game flaws. I remember looking up and seeing they had a nine-point lead with 5:00 to go. I remember thinking, "Don't blow it." I remember shaking my head when J.R. Smith and Kevin Love missed some late jumpers.

3. Anyway, back to the big picture. Obviously, Raptors guard Kyle Lowry was magnificent on his way to 43 points. But I'd give him that step-back jumper used to hit the game-winner any day of the week and twice on Sunday. The Raptors truly are a real threat and shouldn't be taken lightly.

They're better than last season. But they still look like the second-best team in the East, even after beating the Cavs on Friday.

4. I've read that this was a "bad loss" for the Cavs, or that it gives the Raptors some sort of a mental edge ... blah, blah, blah. None of those things are true. Yes, the Cavs blew it. But that's it. Trying to make it sound like anything more than that is silly.

5. Remember, the Raptors won the Atlantic Division each of the past two seasons — then lost in the first round of the playoffs. They were swept by the Wizards last season, despite owning home-court advantage. They have yet to prove they can get it done when it means the most. To me, that's the only "mental edge" involved in a potential Cavs-Raptors series, and it belongs to the Cavs.

6. OK, enough of the rainbows and unicorns. The Cavs can't keep blowing leads. They have to figure out how to get the most out of Kyrie Irving. Too often, he's either dominating the ball too much or scoring 10 points and passing for one assist, as he did Friday.

7. Irving is still learning the difference between being a great individual player (that he is) and playing like a champion. I'd say he's getting closer, but he still has a ways to go. The same holds true of Love. And right there are two of the Big Three.

8. A lot of this falls on Cavs coach Tyronn Lue, and he'll be the first to say so. He's talked about the need for Irving and Love to focus more on winning games and maybe a little less on building "their brand." This may sound stronger than intended. But there is also some truth to it. Lue needs to figure out how to get those two to maximize their talents at winning time. It's one reason why he was hired to replace David Blatt at midseason.

9. LeBron James had a strong game with 25 points, eight rebounds and seven assists. What more is he supposed to do? I guess he could shoot free throws a little better (5-of-9 on Friday). Overall, the Cavs finished 15-of-21. Six misses don't sound all that horrible — until you remember they lost by two.

10. Quick side note: The officiating in this game was atrocious, both ways. (But mostly the Raptors' way.)

11. What we mostly learned from this one is the Cavs are not playing like a championship-caliber club yet. At least, not nearly enough for a team

hoping to win a championship. When things go well, they're certainly up there. They have the talent, and as LeBron indicated when asked about the Joe Johnson sweepstakes, they're plenty good enough as is.

12. But they need to do it for a full 48 minutes. That's the biggest difference between the Cavs and teams like the Warriors and Spurs. Those teams get a lead and never relent — even on the road.

13. Right now, the Cavs (41-16) are two ahead of the Raptors (39-18) for first place in the Eastern Conference, with 25 games to go.

14. Basically, it's time to build good habits, get focused, finish these games and prepare for the playoffs. It's a mindset, and it's about being determined to play together, moving the ball, sticking with the game plan. If the Cavs don't start doing that, well, Joe Johnson, Kevin Johnson, Dennis Johnson, Magic Johnson — it won't matter.

15. Bottom line: Losses like Friday's game happen and the Cavs can still probably beat the Raptors four of seven based on talent alone. But beating the Raptors isn't the primary goal, and the Cavs need to start consistently proving they have bigger aspirations here soon.

FEBRUARY 29

Cavs need Kyrie, Love to get fired up

Random dribbles on the Cavaliers entering Monday's game vs. the Pacers.

1. The good news about the NBA is there's always another game. The bad news is some of the Cavs' flaws were majorly exposed in the previous one vs. the host Wizards on Sunday. And this is the wrong time of year for that.

2. A lot of questions surround Kyrie Irving and Kevin Love and if they're championship-level players — or just really good players. Irving and Love had an opportunity to prove themselves a little with LeBron James resting. They basically did the opposite of that.

3. This isn't intended to trash either player. I thought both played like winners (when healthy) in last season's playoffs. But that doesn't seem to have carried over much. Their overall performances on Sunday make it fair to ask, hey man, how bad do you want it? Where's the leadership? Where's the resolve?

4. Yes, Irving finished with 28 points and six assists — a high number for him. But the Cavs were outscored by a whopping 22 points when he was on the floor. Love had another very pedestrian game with 12 points (4-of-11 shooting) and five rebounds. I don't know much, but I can guarantee you that the Cavs didn't trade for Love or sign him to a max contract because they thought he was "pedestrian."

5. Mostly, this was an opportunity for both players to take a stand with James on the sidelines. They are, after all, two of the supposed Big Three. But they're clearly second and third, and this was their chance to make a case for Nos. 1A and 1B. It was a chance for them to say: "Look, we love LeBron. But we're pretty good, too. We can get it done without him sometimes, too."

6. Tyronn Lue is taking some heat, and some of it is because of the performances of Irving and Love. But you can't keep blaming the coaches. Lue is Irving's fourth coach in just more than four years with the Cavs. Only Byron Scott lasted a full two seasons. The point guard is often referred to as "the coach on the floor." So at some point, some of the blame for the Cavs' failures have to be pinned on the guy with the ball in his hands.

7. Love hasn't nearly been tough enough, either. It's strange to say that about a power forward who averages 11.6 rebounds for his career. There's no question Love is physically tough. There's no question he's remarkably skilled. And there's no question he has yet to consistently put it all together during his time in Cleveland.

8. Another thing I never thought I'd write: I haven't been overly impressed with Tristan Thompson lately. That truly is stunning, because he's the one guy who always gives maximum effort and often keeps the Cavs alive via pure determination. But in the last four games, Thompson is averaging 3.5 points and 7.0 rebounds. The Cavs are paying all that money for that?

9. Lue on the loss: "I thought (Richard Jefferson) played hard. I thought (Timofey Mozgov) kept playing hard and playing tough. That's about it."

10. I'm in agreement with the coach.

11. Of course, J.R. Smith's words were considerably stronger. "We can't do that," he said after Sunday's loss. "If we're serious about who we're supposed to be then we can't do this."

12. Smith added: "If you lose a game like the other night to a team like Toronto and come out here and play the way we did and you had a lack of energy, maybe we shouldn't be in this position."

12. Overall, the Cavs (41-17) have just been too hit-or-miss when the roster suggests they should dominate. That's the frustrating part. Most people would be thrilled with 41 wins at this point — unless they had LeBron, Kyrie, Love and six or seven other pretty doggone good players.

13. In the past week, the Cavs throttled the Thunder in Oklahoma City, came home and lost to the Pistons, blew a big lead in a "statement" game vs. the Raptors on the road, and then got embarrassed by the Wizards. They also beat the Hornets in there. See what I mean by hit or miss?

14. Also in the past week, I've seen new commercials featuring Love or Irving about 25 times apiece. No one has a problem with endorsements. I sure wouldn't suggest pro athletes walk away from money because they aren't living up to the hype. But lately, Irving and Love haven't been.

15. The Cavs have three home games this week and a nice break. After the Pacers on Monday, they get the Wizards again on Friday and the Celtics on Saturday. That's three days off between games. They owe one to each the Wizards and Celtics, as each beat the Cavs at The Q.

16. Friday is also "Miracle of Richfield" night. That team from 1975-76 played with great heart and gave great effort night after thankless night. These Cavs should pay close attention to that team. Because frankly, I'm starting to worry too many of these Cavs don't understand what it will take to be celebrated 40 years from now.

MARCH 1

Cavs finally show needed fight at end

CLEVELAND – Random dribbles from the Cavaliers' 100-96 escape job over the visiting Pacers on Monday.

1. No one gets more agitated than coach Tyronn Lue when he watches the Cavaliers fail to get after it for an entire game. "It's annoying," Lue said. "But when you have a team like we have, with great individual players, they can turn it on at any point."

2. That was certainly the case Monday, when the Cavs sort of lollygagged through a big part of three quarters — then sprung to life when it mattered most. The Pacers aren't playing as well lately as earlier this season. If they had been, things may not have turned out so well for the Cavs

3. But as I wrote in my instant recap, Cavs center Tristan Thompson came up huge at the end — hitting a little hook shot in the lane that broke a late tie. On the next possession, he swatted away a drive by Pacers guard George Hill. Ball game.

4. And if Thompson (14 points, 11 rebounds) keeps playing like this, he'll make a strong case to keep coming off the bench. That's where he returned before the game, with Lue deciding to "mix it up" by starting Timofey Mozgov.

5. While Lue may not have said it, Thompson has undoubtedly struggled lately. In the four games prior to Monday, he was averaging just 3.5 points and 7.0 boards, and seemed to be struggling against bigger opposing centers. It's hard to match his energy off the bench, though, and we saw it vs. the Pacers.

6. Besides that, we hear it time and again: It's not who starts the game, it's who finishes. And Thompson finished with a flurry.

7. Lue on Thompson: "I thought his effort and energy were great. If we can getthat Tristan every night, we're gonna be tough to beat."

8. OK, back to the Cavs and their occasional flick-the-switch mentality. LeBron James definitely couldn't be accused of that Monday, as he went right at the Pacers right away, scoring 33 points after a day of rest. Everyone else? Well ...

9. James also drove and kicked the ball back out to Matthew Dellavedova for a major 3-pointer late. Making those clutch shots shows just how much Delly benefitted from starting in the Finals last season. He was just 1-of-4 on threes at that point, but he made it when it mattered most. And it says a lot that James trusted Dellavedova in that situation.

10. LeBron on the night: "We showed some mental toughness tonight. So many lead changes, so many ties. They grabbed some momentum late in the fourth, but we were able to keep our composure, get some stops, and win the ball game."

11. Kyrie Irving added 20 points and passed for six assists, sinking four important free throws at the end.

12. The day began with a report that Irving wants to move on from the Cavs — but he calmly shot down any such suggestions off after the game. "It's all about winning a championship for Cleveland," he said.

13. The Cavs (42-17) don't play again until Friday, so this will be a nice break. Lue said he plans to rest LeBron a few more times before the end of the regular season, now just about six weeks away.

14. Again, Paul George and the Pacers (31-29) haven't been the same lately — but they play the Cavs tough every time. Read: You may not want to see these guys in the playoffs. "We can play with this team," Pacers coach Frank Vogel said. "We know we can."

MARCH 1

LeBron: Cavs can't worry about Warriors

CLEVELAND — LeBron James says the Cavaliers must work on themselves before worrying about anyone else.

"I don't think we're the group to be looking at other people for motivation," James said after the Cavaliers' win over the Pacers on Monday. "I think we need to figure out and worry about what we got here (rather) than try to use other teams for motivation right now."

That may sound strange coming from the star of a team that's 42-17 and in first place in the Eastern Conference.

But the local and national narrative hasn't focused on the things the Cavs do right. Instead, everything is centered on how the Cavs stack up to teams such as the Spurs, Raptors, Thunder and especially, the defending champion Warriors.

But James threw caution at the idea of the Cavs using opponents — especially ones they're not playing on a given night — as measuring sticks.

"It's a fine line when you're trying to look at other teams and use motivation from that," he said. "Us, we need to continue to work our habits on a daily basis and not worry about (other teams)."

The Cavs don't play again until Friday's home date vs. the Wizards, and don't even practice again until Thursday.

Both James and Kyrie Irving admitted the Cavs are still likely to experience some bumps before they get to the time of the year when it means the most.

Along the way, they'll let the fans and media worry about how they match up with the Warriors and the amazing play of league MVP frontrunner Steph Curry.

"I mean, we don't play Golden State again (in the regular season)," James said. "And if we're fortunate enough to win three rounds in the postseason, which is very hard to do, then it's a possible chance we could see them.

"But we shouldn't be thinking about Golden State right now. We don't play them again. We may not even play them again this season, so that should not be our concern."

7 MIRACLE BREAK

MARCH 4

Cavs of '76 brought life to pro hoops in Cleveland

In 1976, pro basketball was a mere curiosity.

There were no websites rounding up the latest NBA rumors. In fact, there were no websites.

The best time to watch the Finals was on tape delay -- after the local news.

And any thoughts of scream teams or fire-breathing scoreboards or even 3-point lines were still a few years away.

That was particularly the case in Cleveland.

The city had the Browns and Indians, who were struggling at the time.

The Cavaliers?

Well, they existed. But that's about all anyone really knew.

In 1976, if you paid attention to the Cavs, you were a die-hard fan, a rarity, perhaps much like someone who follows pro lacrosse closely today. More likely, you somehow scored free tickets to a game.

THE PLAYERS

The 1975-76 Cavs finished 49-33, which was good enough to win the Central Division.

That alone was news (at least in team headquarters), as this was just the franchise's sixth season of existence.

Up until that point, the Cavs had been sort of an expansion laughingstock.

This team was different, though. It was fairly deep with good balance, and unusually unselfish under coach Bill Fitch -- the only coach the Cavs had ever known.

A whopping seven Cavs averaged double figures in scoring that season, but not one scored more than center Jim Chones' 15.8 a game.

Or get this: The second-leading scorer, forward Campy Russell, came off the bench.

Other top contributors included point guard Jim Cleamons, power forward Jim Brewer, shooting guard Austin Carr, and swingmen Bingo Smith and Dick Snyder. All live on in Cavaliers lore. None were expected to do anything all that special in the postseason.

FIRST-ROUND FRENZY

Today, the NBA postseason consists of 16 teams. Back then, the entire NBA consisted of just 18. The Central Division was made up of the Cavs, Washington Bullets, Houston Rockets, New Orleans Jazz and Atlanta Hawks. The Cavs played home games in the little community of Richfield, their home arena simply known as The Coliseum.

It was in the middle of nowhere then and remains that way today.

But the games that took place in what is now nothing more than a big field, and the men who played them, helped build the Cavs into the must-see production they are today.

It all started in the first round, or what was really the Eastern Conference semifinals, against the Bullets.

The Cavs opened with home-court advantage in Game 1 -- and lost.

But they went to Washington for Game 2 -- and won, by a point. After splitting the next two games, the series was down to a best-of-three, with the Cavs getting two of them in Richfield.

Slowly, people began to notice.

That was especially the case after the Cavs beat the Bullets in Game 5, again, by a single point.

They went to Washington again, and lost again -- this time in overtime. So yes, every game was going down to the wire.

And Game 7 back in Richfield would be no different.

SERVING NOTICE

The teams had two days off between Games 6 and 7, and that's when the big-time buzz around the series truly began.

Suddenly, an entire sports community rallied around the Cavs. They had become all the rage at the barbershop, on the Cleveland sportscasts, in the newspaper headlines.

Cleveland sports fans were starving for a winner, and here was a pro team that had a chance to give them one.

If only it could pull out Game 7 against the defending conference champs.

As most of the others had, the game went back and forth -- not ending until Snyder hit a last-second shot to propel the Cavs to an 87-85 win. The building erupted. Fans stormed the court. The Cavs were moving on.

Now, the Cavs didn't go on to win the title. They didn't even win another round, as Chones broke his foot prior to the next series vs. the Celtics -- deflating the idea that the Cavs would actually have a chance.

But when it came to putting pro basketball on the map in Cleveland, it didn't matter. The Cavaliers were already there.

Despite some dire seasons that followed, they never really left.

And that may really be the true miracle of the 1975-76 Cavaliers. They made their franchise relevant. They made their city and the surrounding communities take notice. They may have downright saved pro basketball in Cleveland.

Basketball hasn't always been king in Cleveland since the Miracle season. But it's always been a talking point. At least, it has since 1976, and you can be sure the 1976 team has everything to do with it.

MARCH 5

No Miracle needed: Cavs play with pace, win

Random dribbles on the Cavaliers' 108-83 hammer job of the visiting Wizards on Friday's "Miracle of Richfield" night.

1. Not a whole lot to be said here other than it looks like the Cavaliers really benefited from three days without a game. They were energized and sharp.

2. Coach Tyronn Lue gave the Cavs a couple days off before everyone returned to practice Thursday. Sometimes, it pays to get a mental break from the game. After all, the Cavs played the mental game Friday as well as at any other time this season.

3. By that, I mean they played smart. They were unselfish, passed the ball, cut to the basket and drove and kicked for open perimeter shots.

4. This is how they need to play every night — especially when it comes to Kyrie Irving. For the first time in a while, he rarely forced anything, and guess what? He still led the team in scoring with a game-high 21 points (to go with a game-high eight assists). Let that be a lesson to everyone: Keep the ball moving, and you'll get it back. And you'll probably be set up for a better look at the basket when you do.

5. People say, "It's just the Wizards," but I'm not buying that. They're one of the East's hottest teams and were riding a four-game winning streak into Friday night. The Wizards are slowly creeping back into the playoff picture and this game was a potential first-round matchup. It was good to send a message.

6. The Wizards blew out the Cavs on Sunday when the Cavs rested LeBron James. The Cavs blew out the Wizards on Friday when the Cavs rested

Kevin Love. What's that tell you? Well, not much — other than the Cavs played the right way and really got after it on defense this time.

7. Iman Shumpert filled in for Love, which was interesting, considering Shumpert is a shooting guard and Love is a power forward. But that moved LeBron into Love's spot and Shumpert into LeBron's spot at small forward. Shumpert just isn't the same, not even defensively, and finished just 0-of-3 shooting for two points. Let's hope he rediscovers his groove soon.

8. Still, it worked out well, as the Cavs flew around the court and created turnovers, which led to some good looks at the hoop and quick, easy scores. Even Timofey Mozgov (14 points) really seemed to enjoy the faster pace. This is what Lue envisioned when he took over for David Blatt at midseason. This is a winning formula, and this team has now shown it can execute it.

9. Love will return to his normal role Saturday vs. the Celtics, and it will be interesting to see if the Cavs can perform with the same pace and space. Not just because Love is back, but because they will almost assuredly be a little more tired after playing the previous night.

10. You can read the rest of my breakdown of things in my quick recap that followed the game. (I too need to save some energy for Saturday.)

11. Finally, what a night for the men on the 1975-76 team. I was alive, but too young to remember much of it beyond having heard the names of Campy Russell, Austin Carr, Jim Chones, Bingo Smith and the others — and even that was several years after the Miracle season.

12. What I cherish even more, though, is the friendships I've developed with Russell and Carr as a member of the FOX Sports Ohio broadcast team. I also had a long conversation with Chones last week, and he's every bit as awesome. These men will be remembered in Cleveland sports history for the rest of time, and deservedly so.

MARCH 6

Cavs seeing benefits of cohesion

CLEVELAND – Random dribbles from the Cavaliers' 120-103 victory over the visiting Celtics on Saturday.

1. Just as you shouldn't get too down after the losses, you shouldn't get too overzealous about the wins. That's a message LeBron James has preached and his teammates have been listening. But the Cavs really displayed some positive signs the past two nights. So it's probably OK for them to at least get a little excited.

2. The Cavaliers are 44-17. Think about. Then think about how so few (outside the locker room) are giving them much of a chance. Now, I would agree — if the Finals were held in early March, the Cavs would be heavy underdogs. But guess when the Finals are actually held? Yep. Late June.

3. In other words, by the time this thing is over, we'll all be wearing Hawaiian shirts, cutoff-jean shorts and fluorescent flip-flops. OK, only I will. But you get the idea. There's still plenty of time.

4. I suspected Iman Shumpert wouldn't stay in his slump forever, and man, what a breakout game he had. Shumpert missed 13 straight shots over a seven-day span entering Saturday, and started to look almost afraid to put it up. But Kevin Love found Shumpert in the corner, wide-open, in the second quarter. Shumpert set his feet, squared up, tucked in the elbow, followed through on the release and buried the corner 3-pointer.

5. As any basketball player will tell you anywhere, sometimes, all you need to do is get that first one out of the way. Sometimes, hitting a basket like that can bring energy to the rest of your game. That sure seemed to be the case for Shumpert. Not only did he finish 4-of-8 from the floor, he grabbed a whopping 16 rebounds.

6. Cavs coach Tyronn Lue smiled widely as he spoke about Shumpert. "He plays like that, we're gonna be tough to beat," Lue said.

7. But Shumpert's big night wasn't just about Shumpert. What was most impressive, and what really says something about how this team is suddenly playing under Lue, is how the Cavs continued to look for Shumpert. They didn't stop giving him the ball or start telling him to just focus on D. Love's pass came with a look. It said, "I believe in you, man. Go for it."

8. I may be overstating there, but that's what I saw. Anyone who plays or watches sports typically can see when guys believe in their teammates – and when they don't. Both situations are pretty obvious. The Cavs know they'll need Shumpert when it means the most. So they know it's in their best interest to get him going.

9. As for the rest of this game, you can read my recap here. The highlights: LeBron scored 28 (with 13 boards), Kyrie Irving had 20, and the Cavs overcame an 18-point deficit to throttle a determined and physical Celtics team. The Cavs are really playing with confidence and pace. People will view them a lot differently if they continue this for another couple weeks.

10. It is indeed interesting how we barely hear anything about the Cavs when they do well – but when they drop a game or two, it's occasionally viewed as mass chaos. ESPN's Dave McMenamin did an excellent job of offering some perspective on that very subject.

11. Again, in the long run, so little of all this stuff will matter if you can make it to June. And as the defending conference champs and owners of the top spot so far this year, the East is the Cavs to lose.

12. There's probably no better example of that than Saturday. The Celtics (38-26) entered the night as the East's third seed. It's admirable how they fight for every inch and play with an edge. Even Lue admitted the Celtics are perhaps the "most physical" team the Cavs will face.

13. Still, the Cavs managed to shoot 51 percent and out-rebound the Celtics by a 47-37 count. The Cavs also held a whopping 52-34 scoring advantage in the paint. So if the Celtics are truly tough, the Cavs sure haven't backed down.

14. Finally, next week will tell us considerably more about where the Cavs may be headed — and if their recent habits of moving the ball and clamping down defensively are sustainable. After Monday's home game vs. the Grizzlies, it's off to Sacramento, Los Angeles and Utah for the final Western swing of the season. The road is never easy — it can, however, offer a darn good team another chance to believe it's becoming great.

MARCH 8

Cavs call it bad, and they're right

CLEVELAND – Random dribbles on the Cavaliers' 106-103 stunner of a loss to the visiting Grizzlies on Monday.

1. How does this happen? That's what I kept asking myself after this one. If you remember, the Cavs throttled the Grizzlies in Memphis in the Grizzlies' season-opener. And I mean throttled them.

2. The difference between that late-October game and this? Well, the Grizzlies' best players sat in this out. Mike Conley, Zach Randolph, Matt Barnes and Marc Gasol (who's been out) weren't on the floor. But I'm not going to harp on that. This is the NBA. Anyone can beat anyone, anywhere and anytime.

3. What puzzles me more is why the Cavs don't come out and just take it right at a team that's licking its wounds. I'm sure part of it is the Cavs know they can turn it on. They're at home against an inferior team. No deficit is too daunting. At least, that seemed to be the mindset.

4. Not to make excuses, but frankly, it's easy to get caught up in that type of thinking when you have so much talent. The Cavs may not always play like the East's best team, but they're still 44-18 and in first place. They're still favored to represent the conference in the Finals — and no disrespect to the Raptors, Celtics or Heat, but the Cavs are still favored by nearly a landslide.

5. Part of me wonders if that can be a problem. Maybe the Cavs would be more focused if they (or anyone else) thought they had a real challenger in the East. Instead, everyone seems to be predicting the Warriors or Spurs will win the championship — and the Cavs will just sort of be in the Finals, too. But without a doubt, most everyone is predicting the East representative will be the Cavs.

6. As I wrote in my recap, along with lacking focus, the Cavs looked slow, clunky, out of sorts. They went just 7-of-29 on 3-pointers. Kevin Love and J.R. Smith combined to shoot 4-of-20 overall. And other than LeBron James (28 points, nine rebounds), I'd say only Tristan Thompson (11 points, 5-of-6 shooting) made the most of his minutes.

7. Yes, I know Kyrie Irving scored 20 of his 27 points in the second half.

But he also committed seven turnovers on the night — compared to four assists. Irving is a talented scorer and can be a very determined floor leader when he wants. But something just seems "off" with him too often this season. At least, it does compared to the Irving we've seen in the past.

8. Cavs coach Tyronn Lue: "I just thought they were tougher than we were. They played hard and out-scrapped us."

9. More Lue, on the season-high 25 turnovers: "It looked really bad. We just didn't have a good feel for the ball."

10. Some nights, the Cavs actually do play with the pace and spacing Lue envisioned. Others, they only use it in spurts. Then there are games like Monday, where they don't do it all night, then resort to "hero ball," at the end. The problem was, it almost worked. So that makes it easy for that dangerous habit to continue.

11. LeBron put it this way: "I can say we're a team that's ready to start the playoffs tomorrow, but we're not. We're still learning. We still have things that happen on the court that just, that shouldn't happen."

12. Love also offered an interesting take: "We just could have done a better job of respecting the game. A team like that, they were going to come out and swing for the fences, and they did. That was a real bad loss for us."

13. LeBron, Love, Lue … all made some strong points. Basically, these aren't exactly the things you want to be talking about with the playoffs a little more than a month away.

14. The Cavs now hit the road for seven of eight, beginning with a four-game West swing Wednesday at Sacramento. This is a good opportunity for the Cavs to put this behind them, play like they know they can, and start pulling it together on a more consistent basis. Otherwise, they might just get the competition in the East that no one really, truly believes they have.

MARCH 9

Cavs must use West swing to sing

Random dribbles on the Cavaliers heading into Wednesday's game at the Kings.

1. Following last year's back-to-back wins in Los Angeles vs. the Lakers and Clippers, the Cavs went 34-9 to finish the regular season. Count the Eastern Conference playoffs, and it's 50-11.

2. That LA stop was also the start of a 12-game winning streak.

3. Last season's Cavs arrived in Los Angeles with occasional bouts of inconsistency and frustration, and once-in-a-while rumors of team discord. Sound familiar?

4. This season's Cavs looked cohesive and determined in weekend wins over the Wizards and Celtics. Two nights later, they flopped against a vastly undermanned Grizzlies team — at home.

5. Along the way, there's been talk about Kyrie Irving wanting to leave Cleveland (he's refuted), talk about LeBron James wanting to leave Cleveland (let's hope he doesn't even bother to address), and talk about LeBron tweeting things that none of us really understand — and thing that he may not want us to understand.

6. For the record, I'm OK with all of the above. I mean, honestly. Who knows, who cares, and despite all the freaking out, the Cavs are 44-18 and in first place in the East.

7. Still, as I've written and said in a recent podcast, not everything is dandy with the Cavs. They clearly have enough talent to overcome some of their issues — but those issues exist nonetheless.

8. For one, the ball movement isn't always what it should be. Against the Grizzlies, they didn't defend for large portions of the game. Sometimes, Irving looks like a guy who has yet to place winning above all else. Other times, Kevin Love looks like a guy who's too content to just vanish into thin air.

9. Those two aren't the Cavs' biggest problems. They're just two of the three (after LeBron) who need to deliver on an almost-every-night basis.

And by "deliver," I don't mean scoring a bunch of points. I mean leading the rest of the team in being aggressive, playing the right way, and as Love himself talked about the other night, "respecting the game."

10. Perhaps the biggest issue is maddening inconsistency. We saw it vs. the Celtics and Wizards. So what's it say when the Cavs can't do it against a Grizzlies team that's missing four of five starters? To me, it says an entire lack of effort and focus. And that's happened too often with these Cavs.

11. Anyway, back to LA. The Cavs play the Lakers on Thursday, the Clippers on Sunday. The numbers show what the Cavs did after beating those two on their (shared) home floor last season. They came together. They ripped through the rest of the league. They left their troubles in the dust.

12. Now, the Cavs are back out West. They're healthy. They have the same main players from last season. They need to remember what happened last year in Los Angeles, and do it again. They need to use LA as a reminder of how to be the team they say they are. It's worked before. It can again.

MARCH 10

For a night, Cavs get it entirely right

Random dribbles on the Cavaliers' 120-111 victory over the host the Kings on Wednesday.

1. So much happened in this game, it's hard to know where to begin. That will happen when two teams combine for 231 points. There was some ugliness, but mostly, lots of great offense.

2. One highlight: When Kyrie Irving drove for back-to-back, and-one layups, completed over Kings rookie Willie Cauley-Stein each time. Irving is 6-foot-3 (on a good day). Stein is a 7-footer. But Irving went right at him, got fouled, and spun the ball through the basket — twice. Cauley-Stein complained to the refs, but that was probably just to hide some of the embarrassment.

3. Irving went just 3-of-10 on 3-pointers, but the three he made were pretty memorable. Irving also seemed to bury each right when the Cavs really needed it.

4. Kyrie finished with 30 points, and LeBron James had 25 and 11 rebounds — and that almost seemed like a footnote when you consider some of the other brilliant performances. But James had an amazing and-one finish of his own, and in the event you ever wonder why people always buy his jersey, it's shots like those that explain it. It was a great night for everyone else, a good night for LeBron.

5. Another highlight, of course: The fact Kevin Love (17 points, 10 boards) was again miserable on 3-pointers, and then swished the biggest shot of the night. It came off a feed from Irving, and it thwarted the Kings' attempt to rally. As you know, Love was fouled on the shot and knocked down the ensuing free throw, scoring four points off one stroke from the corner.

6. Love on the shot: "My teammates told me to keep shooting. Now they're laughing at me."

7. But the Cavs were only "laughing" because Love was in the middle of an interview and they wanted to have a little fun at his expense. As Irving told FOX Sports Ohio, wins like this to start a four-game trip are a great way to "build some camaraderie."

8. Tristan Thompson (18 points, 15 rebounds) was simply magnificent. No one should ever have to go up against Kings mammoth and ultra-skilled center DeMarcus Cousins for 37 minutes. But that's what Thompson did, as the Cavs were without the ill Timofey Mozgov. Yes, Cousins finished with 29 points and 11 rebounds — but Thompson made his presence felt, as Cousins finished 8-of-22 from the floor.

9. J.R. Smith (15 points) also hit a big three near the end, and while he too was up-and-down for a lot of the game, he played hard and didn't force too much, if anything.

10. It wasn't all rainbows and unicorns, of course. The Cavs did allow a four-point halftime deficit to expand to 11 in the third quarter. They also gave up too many points, especially in the first half (60). But if they play with this type of energy and pace, they can be a fun and winning team.

11. Actually, the Cavs (45-18) are already a winning team. But if they can bring some real joy into that locker room, they're going places, and maybe further than you think.

8 STRETCH & RUN

MARCH 11

Cavs beginning to see value of sharing

Random dribbles on the Cavaliers' 120-108 win over Kobe and the host Lakers on Thursday.

1. Well, that was everything it was expected to be — easy. Aside from a few throwback moments from Kobe Bryant, the Lakers were barely even there. I love Bryon Scott personally, but his teams just don't defend.

2. That said, I feel bad for Scott. He's willingly put himself in some losing situations, and in losing situations, the fall guy is always the coach. I'd be surprised if he's back next season, and it may be time to start thinking about the college ranks if you're Scott.

3. Anyway, on to the Cavs (46-18). These aren't the most quality opponents, mind you, but the Cavs raced past the Kings on Wednesday and were never threatened by the Lakers. They scored exactly 120 points in each game.

4. That's basically what you're looking for on a four-game trip out West. You won the first two and suddenly, most everything seems fine again.

5. And what a start for Channing Frye, huh? He filled in for the injured Kevin Love (knee) and erupted to the tune of 21 points on 8-of-10 shooting. That included 5-of-7 on 3-pointers. He also grabbed seven rebounds.

6. That's more than the Cavs expect from even Love, frankly. It's certainly more than they've been getting from him – and Love could learn a little bit about Frye's performance. Just relax, square up, shoot the ball and have some doggone fun.

7. Still, this isn't intended to pick on anyone, as Love buried the game's biggest shot in the win over the Kings. Rather, it's to show the professionalism of Frye, staying ready and making himself available to

shoot despite his regular lack of playing time.

8. Meanwhile, Kyrie Irving appears to be getting more comfortable with each game — looking more and more like the All-Star point guard we all knew before his offseason knee surgery. Irving finished with 26 points, and has now scored more than 20 in seven straight games.

9. Irving has truly amazed the past two games with his driving and spinning layups off the backboard with either hand in traffic. As Campy Russell pointed out on FOX Sports Ohio, Irving still needs to do a better job of getting other people involved and stop using so many dribbles to get where he wants to go. But the Cavs also need Kyrie to score — a lot.

10. LeBron James finished with 24 points in his fun duel with Bryant, but it was James' driving and kicking that was most impressive. His penetration led to a lot of those open jumpers for Frye, J.R. Smith (17 points) and Matthew Dellavedova (11).

11. Lousy opponent or not, the Cavs moved the basketball, and won. They need to do that every game, and especially, against the really good teams when it's not always easy. They have to know by now that it leads to much more balance and better looks at the basket.

12. And when the Cavs get good looks and knock them down — well, they're unbeatable. Know what their record is in the previous 47 games when they shoot 50 percent or better? Yeah. Try 47-0.

13. Kyrie to FOX Sports Ohio on the Cavs: "It's just about us. We have to lock in. We have to do it for 48 minutes. We all have to hold each other accountable."

14. And the Cavs and their fans all give a hearty amen.

15. Finally, it's hard to believe this was the final time the Cavs will face Bryant. He truly had one of those throwback nights, scoring 26 points on a remarkable 11-of-16 points. Over-the-hill or not, Bryant always knows how to rise to the occasion. Kudos, Kobe. We're gonna miss ya.

16. Kyrie on the final meeting with Bryant: "It's emotional, knowing the impact he's had. It was great to play against him one last time."

17. The Cavs will remain in Los Angeles, take Friday off, practice Saturday, and then face the Clippers on Sunday.

MARCH 14

Trip to West bringing out Cavs' best

Random dribbles on the Cavaliers' 114-90 hammer job of the host Clippers on Sunday.

1. It's not quite time to crown the Cavs NBA champions, but when they play with this type of pace and space (and knock down those 3-pointers), they sure can be good. Like, awesome.

2. It seems as if that awful home loss to the undermanned Grizzlies was six months ago — as the Cavs are 3-0 on the West Coast swing heading into Monday's final stop at Utah. They've averaged a whopping 118 points on the trip.

3. Part of it has to do with the Cavs just being more focused. Part of it has been the improved (and considerably more fluid) play of Kyrie Irving. Part of it is because the Cavs are finally making some perimeter shots.

4. This is a team that can be lethal in April, May and June if the guys who are supposed to be able to shoot well actually do it. LeBron James and Kevin Love have struggled on 3-pointers all year. If just one of them gets hot from the perimeter, the Cavs will typically be very tough to beat. If both do at the same time, it's probably lights out, and I don't care who you are.

5. Love was 0-of-4 on threes vs. the Clippers — but James was 3-of-4. Overall, the Cavs were 18-of-37 from beyond the arc and they handed the Clippers their worst loss of the season.

6. Thirty-seven threes is probably too many. Unless, of course, you're making them. And man, the Cavs sure made them. James finished with 27 points, and Irving and J.R. Smith (5-of-8 on threes) added 17 apiece.

7. And it sure looks like Channing Frye (15 points on 5-of-7 threes) is going to be a steal if he continues at his LA pace. He buried both the Lakers and Clippers, and right now, he's playing better than Love.

8. But Love just needs to keep shooting. He could afford to pull it together a little in other areas as well, and get his confidence back — but few things build a basketball player's faith more than making shots. I have a feeling once Love gets going, he won't stop. He just needs to rediscover his stroke before, say, June.

9. Cavs coach Tyronn Lue summarized the game this way: "Channing coming out and making those threes kind of became contagious. LeBron set the tone early with his pace, getting rebounds, pushing it. It wasn't all for himself. He got the other guys involved making shots."

10. People who accuse the Cavs (47-18) of occasionally lacking cohesion and a championship mentality should take a look at the Clippers. My goodness. Yes, they were again without the injured Blake Griffin. But I never thought I'd see a Doc Rivers-coached team appear so fragile. So much talent, so little living up to it.

11. LeBron on the win: "We're getting into form right now. We've got a great rotation going right now. The guys are healthy and we're just trying to play the game the right way."

12. If it continues, with some real consistency, this team is going to make the postseason even more interesting.

MARCH 15

Too many J's result in 'L' for Cavs

Random dribbles on the Cavaliers' ugly 94-85 loss to the host Jazz on Monday.

1. The Cavs just didn't feel like playing — or least not playing the right way for long enough. They didn't really run an offense They didn't really rotate defensively, and they sure didn't take anything but shots that weren't about to drop.

2. Meanwhile, the Jazz got some terrific looks, looks that couldn't have been any better. But every Cavs shot appeared difficult. Part of that was the Jazz defense. Part of it was the Cavs' unwillingness to fight extra hard on an off shooting night.

3. LeBron James (23 points, 12 rebounds) always plays hard. So do Tristan Thompson and Matthew Dellavedova — although neither had the numbers to support it. As for too many other Cavs? Well, that's sometimes debatable. That's been one of the concerns with this team: How bad do they want it on a nightly basis?

4. The Cavs were 10-of-42 of 3-pointers. That came a day after an 18-of-37 performance in a blowout win over the Clippers. As Austin Carr said on the FOX Sports Ohio broadcast: "If you're gonna live by the three, you're gonna die by the three."

5. Basically, this was a case of the Cavs having tired legs after three straight road games — and not doing what was needed to push through it.

6. Still, you can't complain too loudly about a West swing that ended 3-1. Frankly, you can't really complain at all. These losses happen. What's important is the Cavs don't just accept them.

7. Yes, the Warriors are viewed as a team that "lives" by the 3-pointer. And that is true to a certain extent. But they also pass, cut and find the open man near the basket, and they do it every bit as much as they launch from the perimeter. That's something the Cavs did not do Monday.

8. Kyrie Irving (17 points) and J.R. Smith (five) were particularly brutal from the floor. Irving went just 7-of-23 and Smith 2-of-12. The two also combined for 2-of-17 shooting on threes. On the bright side, Chris Haynes of cleveland.com reported Irving was still working and putting up shots after the game.

9. Cavs coach Tyronn Lue to reporters: "It was just one of those games. We tried to fight, we tried to compete. We just didn't have it."

10. As an aside, Channing Frye and Jazz forward Trey Lyles were booted for a dust-up in the second half, when Frye received a Lyles elbow where it counts, and reacted. The fact Frye got ejected was ridiculous — especially after officials took 15 minutes to review the play. I angrily tweeted something about the whole process, but it's Lue's opinion that counts.

11. Lue on the refs' extra-long review: "How many times you gotta see it? Just call what you're gonna call and let's move on."

12. Anyway, back to the game. The Cavs only shot eight free throws all night. Eight. That's perhaps the biggest sign the Cavs were not aggressive, not trying to get to the basket, and settled way too often. Almost half of the Cavs' 88 shots were threes.

13. Kevin Love (12 points, nine boards) is averaging just 13.8 points and 9.8 rebounds in his previous four games. He's shooting 34 percent from the floor and 18 percent from beyond the arc. The Cavs have done OK in this

stretch, so when he finally picks it up — well, that will be a huge bonus. He just doesn't seem confident right now.

14. LeBron on the loss: "We definitely settled for the outside shot too much tonight. We had some good looks, but you gotta recognize when it's not going down, and try to get to the paint a little more and try to create some opportunities."

15. The Jazz were without Gordon Hayward, their best all-around player who was out with a foot injury. Shooting guard Rodney Hood (28 points) more than made up for it. Minus Hayward, the Jazz aren't all that great. But they sure play smart and play hard, and sure out-worked the Cavs on this night.

16. The Cavs (47-19) are still 2.5 games ahead of the Raptors for first place in the East. The Raptors lost at home to the Bulls on Monday. Interestingly, the Bulls are now in the No. 8 spot. If the playoffs started today, that's who the Cavs would face in the first round.

MARCH 17

Minus LeBron, Cavs find way to escape

CLEVELAND — Random dribbles from the Cavaliers' 99-98 squeaker of a win over the visiting Mavericks on Wednesday.

1. Oh, what life might be like without LeBron James. For the record, the Cavs are 4-12 in games without LeBron the past two seasons. But the only one they care about is that No. 4.

2. There were times the Cavs moved the ball, defended and rebounded like champions. There were other times you were hoping they could land LSU star Ben Simmons in the lottery.

3. How else do you explain the fact the Cavs blew a 20-point lead — twice. And remember, we're talking about one game here.

4. Kyrie Irving was at times brilliant, at times maddening, and most of the time, somewhere in between. Irving scored 33 points, and while it may seem like his 28 shots were too many, Cavs coach Tyronn Lue asked Irving to score. And Irving did. A lot. In the end, the Cavs needed every last point.

5. It's true that Kyrie finished with just one assist. And even that only happened because Kevin Love buried a corner 3-pointer. But I wouldn't be too hard on Irving. The Cavs had at least six or seven wide open shots off Irving passes that didn't drop. Can't blame the point guard for that.

6. Love gave one of his better performances of the season, scoring 23 points with 18 rebounds. I recently mentioned that Love needs to start rebounding like a madman again. He was much more aggressive, much more fiery, much more … well, in tune with how he needed to play to win.

7. Love can be a little soft, and I don't mean his willingness to mix it up underneath. I'm referring to demanding the ball and calling out his teammates when they don't deliver. That's actually understandable. Nobody wants to come across as a jerk or a distraction. But there's nothing wrong with getting into position, calling for the ball and making it clear that if you don't have a shot, your teammate will get it back.

8. He seemed to exhibit those characteristics Wednesday and it served him well.

9. Tristan Thompson is one guy who never seems to get many shots when James rests, and that didn't change on this night. Thompson was just 0-of-2 for 0 points. He did grab eight rebounds and was relentless on the boards, and honestly, that's why he's out there. Read: He was huge without scoring a point.

10. Iman Shumpert also started (in place of LeBron) and took just two shots. The Cavs would probably like to see Sumpert get going offensively, at least a little bit. He's struggled shooting and almost looks a little timid. But defensively, he's been as good as ever, especially over the past week or so.

11. It may not be a popular thing to say, but it appears the Cavs won the Channing Frye trade. Not popular because they gave up Anderson Varejao to pull it off. But Frye (14 points, 5-of-7 shooting) really opens things up for the offense. When he misses a 3-pointer, it's actually a surprise. I'm not so sure you can say that about anyone else on the team.

12. Kyrie on playing without LeBron: "Honestly, it was a personal challenge. We know what the record is (without James). I know I took it personally and I have to lead the team whether he's in or out."

13. If you think the Cavs (48-19) can be maddening, wait until you get a

load of the Mavs (34-34). They're a veteran team, a well-coached team, and they seem to be on a mission not to make the playoffs. One thing they aren't is a good rebounding team. That seems to be hurting them recently, as they've lost five of six with two of their next four against the Warriors. Good luck with all that.

14. The Cavs hit the road again, and it's vital they play well at the Magic on Friday. Winning Saturday against Dwyane Wade and the Heat in their building will be a tall task.

MARCH 18

All that matters is what Cavs are doing in June

CLEVELAND -- It's serious business time for the Cavaliers, and it's fair to ask if they yet have a true identity.

The short answer is no. Not as much of one as they'd like anyway.

But they are getting closer to being the team they say they are, the force they believe they can still become.

It may sound strange to imply a team with a 48-19 record is suffering from an identity crisis and is something other than a juggernaut.

Then again, this is a different season. Everyone is comparing the Cavs to the Warriors and Spurs. And right now, neither of those teams has a match.

The Warriors and Spurs are unbeatable at home. They're blowing opponents out of just about any arena -- home or road. Both teams are making a push for 70 (or more) wins.

The Cavs, on the other hand, are just winning.

And when they lose, it's often presented as some sort of a major malfunction -- as if the Cavs are somehow in disarray because they got beat. Truth is, losing rarely happens. It just happens a little more often than it does to the two powers out West.

With 15 games remaining, the Cavs lead the Raptors by 2.5 games for first place in the Eastern Conference. LeBron James, Kyrie Irving and Kevin Love are healthy. In fact, so is every other key member of the roster.

Last season, the Cavs finished on 32-9 tear -- but they still didn't gain the top seed heading into the playoffs. They won the East anyway. They did it without Love for all but three games of the postseason. They did it with a hobbled Irving at about 40 percent (and zero percent in the final five games of the Finals).

This year, the Cavs are in a much better spot. But because of the success of the Warriors and Spurs, everyone on the outside seems to behave as if the Cavs are playing for third.

Why? Because they're not getting it done any certain way. They don't always do it with defense. They don't always do it with grace. They don't always do it with great ball movement. They don't always do it by large margins. And sometimes, they struggle with -- or even lose to -- considerably inferior opponents.

Those are real drawbacks, and they shouldn't be ignored. But they're also things that can be overcome when it means the most.

Are the Cavs as good as the Warriors and Spurs right now? No.

Do they only need to be better than one of them for a couple of weeks in June? That's really all that matters.

"Just get me to the playoffs," James has been known to say. In fact, he spoke those very words last year, when the Cavs started 19-20 and lacked anything resembling unity.

Well, LeBron and the Cavs got to the playoffs. And they emerged from the East in spite of all the (alleged) drama.

Anyway, back to their identity.

What type of team are they under new coach Tyronn Lue? To what do they turn when things seems bleak? How will they ever beat the Warriors or Spurs, without home court-advantage, in a seven-game series?

Today, those questions aren't so easy to answer.

That's why the Cavs have some things to still figure out in these final three weeks of the regular season. But if this year is anything like last, they will.

It's all that mattered before and it's all that will matter again.

MARCH 20

Latest Cavs loss shows lack of grit

Random dribbles on the Cavaliers' 122-101 despicable defeat to the host Heat on Saturday.

1. Oh, brother. That's all I could say as I rolled my eyes and watched the Cavaliers allow themselves to get dismantled by a Heat team that, frankly, was just more interested in playing basketball.

2. I'm not going to write too much about this one, though. If the Cavs can take the night off, then by golly, so can I.

3. Part of me was willing to give the Cavs a pass. A loss here was understandable. It was the Cavs' fifth game in seven days, and the second of a back-to-back on the road — against a playoff-ready team, no less. But

wouldn't it be nice if the Cavs actually won a game where everything was set up for them to lose?

4. Or wouldn't it be nice if they at least competed? I know, I know. Tired legs and all that. And again, the Heat are no joke. But come on, man. You need to come out and at least act like champions. In losses to teams such as the severely decimated Grizzlies (at home) and the young Trail Blazers and … well, the list goes on.

5. Basically, the Cavs just have too many ugly, disheartening defeats for a team with championship aspirations. This was another.

6. LeBron James was just fine, scoring 26 points on 13-of-20 shooting in three quarters. But where were Kevin Love, J.R. Smith, Iman Shumpert and Tristan Thompson?

7. Kyrie Irving (14 points, 5-of-8 shooting) wasn't quite as invisible as those guys, but he wasn't all there, either. He didn't really help the cause or play a winning game — as the Cavs were outscored by 21 with Irving on the floor.

8. And blame whoever you want, but Love needs to start putting up max-contract performances on a regular basis. He does, after all, have a max contract.

9. Love's up-and-down season has been blamed on everything from LeBron to Kyrie to the coaches to Love himself, to probably the political conventions and maybe even the Pope. But who knows, who cares, and stop forcing people to make excuses for you. Just get it together.

10. The Cavs fell to 49-20. They won't be breaking the Bulls' all-time record. The playoffs can't get here soon enough. This team just doesn't seem interested enough in the regular season.

MARCH 21

More Love will make the Cavs feel better

Quick random dribbles on the Cavaliers entering Monday's game vs. the Nuggets.

1. The Cavs are saying Kevin Love (sick) may not play. Love missed his second straight shootaround. He also missed the one Saturday prior to the

game vs. the Heat. He played in that game, but in theory only.

2. Love doesn't seem to be as mentally tough now as he was with the Timberwolves. I am strictly using the eye test for that. But he seemed to really enjoy playing the game in Minnesota — which is one reason why the Cavs traded for him. Now? It seems like it's become just a job. I don't know this for certain, but Love seems to need to rediscover his love of the game.

3. The guy can still be absolutely invaluable, and if he played on a team where he was the first or second option, he'd still be considered a top two power forward. The Cavs just haven't figured out how to maximize Love next to LeBron James and Kyrie Irving — and Love hasn't figured it out, either.

4. Love is averaging 15.6 points and 9.9 rebounds. Those numbers should be closer to 18 and 11. Part of it is because Love hasn't shot the ball well this season. But that doesn't explain the dip in rebounding. He's just not consistently been as aggressive.

5. The Cavs (49-20) now hold just a one-game lead over the Raptors for first place in the East. Not a huge concern, as the Raptors owned home-court advantage in the first round and a top three seed in each of the past two years — and lost in the first round both times, anyway.

6. What would be a concern is if the Cavs lost the top seed because they played poorly. Last thing you want is to look bad entering mid-April. Overall, the Cavs have just been slightly better than so-so since the All-Star break.

7. Either way, this team is hardly panicked. Both the Cavs and Spurs are strong believers that you don't need to break regular-season records to win when it means the most. The Warriors may have overextended themselves. At least, that's what other top contenders are hoping. We'll know who is right in late June. For now, the Cavs just need to worry about themselves and start building better habits.

MARCH 22

Despite talk, not all is bad for Cavs

CLEVELAND – Random dribbles from the Cavaliers' 124-91 dismantling of the visiting Nuggets on Monday.

1. The Cavs were supposed to win this game by about 30 points and they did even better than that. Imagine if they hadn't blown that 19-point lead in the first half.

2. LeBron James was again magnificent, compiling a triple-double (33 points, 11 rebounds, 11 assists) and forcing me to Google the words "Jusuf Nurkic."

3. Turns out Nurkic is the Nuggets' backup center. He blocked a James shot then immediately talked a little trash. Bad idea, kid. Nurkic is 7-foot and 280 pounds — but LeBron spent the rest of the night making the poor guy feel considerably smaller.

4. Other than that, much of the talk after this game centered on Cavs forward Channing Frye (14 points, 5-of-9 shooting) — who started in place of the ill Kevin Love. Obviously, Frye has been a nice fit since arriving in a February trade with the Magic.

5. Now, let's not get ahead of ourselves. I'm not about to imply Frye is as good of a player as Love. But Frye is doing some things that Love is not at the moment. For one, Frye is relaxed out there, not forcing anything while consistently knocking down perimeter shots. He is making the most of his minutes and stretching opposing defenses.

6. Frye is also occasionally going strong to the basket and finishing — something for which he wasn't known in previous stops. He's playing with confidence, playing smart, and giving the Cavs a real lift.

7. In the past five games, Frye is averaging 10.4 points on 59 percent shooting in 20 minutes. In that same stretch, Love is averaging 14.0 points on 43 percent shooting in 27 minutes. Frye is hitting 52 percent of his 3-pointers; Love 36 percent.

8. Love is clearly the superior rebounder (he's grabbing 8.5 to Frye's 3.0 in the past five games). But overall, Frye just seems to be more in the flow of things, more readily open, less mechanical and appears less concerned with

making mistakes.

9. Unlike Love, it seems as if Frye feels no pressure. No one expects a whole lot from Frye. So if he doesn't do much, it's barely noticed. Love, on the other hand ...

10. Cavs coach Tyronn Lue on Frye: "We have to continue to use him. We have a great roster, we have great bigs. Every night, he's going to play. Depending on how the flow of the game goes, he'll play more minutes."

11. Still, there is of hope for Love when it comes to maximizing his role. He was at his very best last season in the three playoff games vs. the Celtics (before getting injured).

12. Perhaps watching Frye will give Love a better idea of how to approach things. Basically, Frye always looks comfortable next to James and Kyrie Irving. Love only looks comfortable sometimes. At other times, he looks downright miserable.

13. Anyway, enough of all that. The Cavs have officially won the Central Division and 50 games. Still, no 50-20 team in history has been this scrutinized, and oftentimes ridiculed, by members of the media and fans.

14. Sure, the Cavs have their issues — but they've won nine of 12 and are still the team to beat in the Eastern Conference. Of course, I turned on two different national sports networks after the game and actually heard the following sentence: "No one in the East is afraid of the Cavs."

15. Excuse me while I throw my remote through the television.

16. First, this is pro basketball. No one admits they fear anyone. Second, what those so-called experts actually mean is no one respects the Cavs. They're wrong about that, too. But whatever.

17. Also, the pundits are leaving out the following truth: The Cavs couldn't possibly care less about random opinions. They believe the national perception is slanted. Other than James and maybe Irving, they aren't exactly a splashy team. Without question, that impacts how the Cavs are covered overall and analyzed on social media.

18. More importantly, the Cavs believe they can beat anyone in the East in a seven-game series right now — and they're not even at their best. So afraid? Brave? Taunting LeBron when you block his shot on a Monday night in

March? Trust me, none of it matters.

19. Another thing everyone seems to forget: The NBA has always been a superstar-driven league. Name a team in the East with a bigger star than James. I know. I can't do it, either.

20. Again, I'm not here to tell you the Cavs are playing championship-level basketball. They're not. But not afraid of LeBron James? Well, here's some free advice: You'd better get afraid.

21. LeBron on winning the Central: "Along the journey you never want to take things for granted and accomplishments that happen along the way. You've got to take it in. It's not given every year, obviously, that you can win a division title, win 50 games in a league where it's so hard to win. ... It's a pretty cool thing."

MARCH 24

Cavs show how O ought to go

CLEVELAND – Random dribbles from the Cavaliers' 113-104 win over the visiting Bucks.

1. Offensively, the Cavaliers were sharp and aggressive for most of the game. They played with great confidence, and no less than a clearly determined LeBron James (26 points) led the way.

2. After a game off feeling ill, Kevin Love (24 points, 10 rebounds) looked entirely re-energized. He shot the ball well (8-of-14) and played with a little bounce in his step.

3. When that happens, the Cavs typically win — because when Love is missing shots, it's hard to say the Cavs actually have a Big Three. It's more like James, Kyrie Irving and another guy who may or may not join in.

4. Love still took too many 3-pointers for my liking. But most of his 10 shots from beyond the arc were good looks. He made four, and hey, 40 percent sure is better than the past few weeks. So, no complaints.

5. As I tweeted prior to the game (and shamelessly stole from Jeff Phelps), Love has taken 18 or 19 shots seven times this season. In those games, he's averaging 25 points and 12 rebounds. The Cavs are 6-1 in those games.

6. And yes, I'm allowed to shamelessly steal stuff from Phelps. We grew up on the same street, we were the best man at each other's weddings, and we now co-host a weekly TV show together. It's been a nice run for two dorks from Cuyahoga Falls, Ohio.

7. Anyway, the reason I threw out the Love numbers wasn't to draw any sort of conclusion — or to imply the Cavs should center the offense around him. It was merely to show that when Love is aggressive, and the Cavs get him shots, good things happen.

8. Irving scored 16 points in what was truly one of his finer performances of the season. He also passed for eight assists and grabbed eight rebounds. It was a heady game for the Cavs point guard, who was celebrating his 24th birthday.

9. One opposing GM told me a few weeks ago he thinks the Cavs are at their best when the shot-taking pecking order is James, Love and then Irving. Or at least when Love and Irving attempt around the same amount of shots. In those situations, Irving becomes more of a distributor, more of a "true" point guard who facilitates the offense and sets up others.

10. That was the Irving we saw against the Bucks.

11. LeBron on the offense as of late: "It's great basketball. Everyone's in a great rhythm. The ball is moving … and it's just good ball."

12. The Cavs (51-20) have won 10 of 13. Yes, the defense needs work. Yes, they've still been a little too hit-or-miss. But they seem to be picking up some steam and showing some good signs with just three weeks left in the regular season.

13. Giannis Antetokounmpo is really starting to make basketball magic Bucks. My goodness, that guy is scary on the floor. The Bucks have been a disappointment after making the playoffs last season. In fact, lots of Bucks fans gave me grief when I ranked them ninth in the East in my preseason power rankings. I haven't heard from those fans since.

14. It's now off to New York — as the Cavs visit the Nets on Thursday and Carmelo Anthony and the Knicks on Saturday. If the Cavs can keep playing like this, and pick it up on D, more good things will result.

MARCH 25

Cavs other two must join LeBron soon

Lots of random dribbles on the Cavaliers' ugly 104-95 road loss to the Nets on Thursday.

1. Losses like this make me wonder about the stars on this team not named LeBron James. That means you, Kyrie Irving and Kevin Love.

2. Sometimes, I wonder if Irving and Love have enough mental toughness to overcome those nights (like Thursday) when the shots aren't falling. Don't get me wrong. I understand this is a shot-making league. And if you can't knock 'em down, eventually, you're doomed. Unless, of course, you find other ways to stay strong and rattle the opponent.

3. Irving, Love and J.R. Smith missed a lot of wide-open looks Thursday. Again, that's gonna happen. But again, what do you do to overcome it when the basketball gods are apparently against you? For Irving and Love, I'm afraid the answer is too often not enough.

4. This isn't to excuse the rest of the Cavs not named LeBron. And I'm not here to bury Irving and Love. But the Cavs outside of the Big Three … well, they're mostly role players.

5. Role players aren't supposed to carry you. They're supposed to supplement the stars. They're supposed to play their best basketball at home. They're expected to struggle on the road. And Smith, Tristan Thompson, Iman Shumpert, Matthew Dellavedova and Channing Frye did indeed struggle Thursday.

6. That is when James, Irving and Love need to deliver. It's why teams want big names in the first place — to carry you when the supporting cast falls short. But Thursday, only James (30 points, 13-of-16 shooting) came through. He did more than enough.

7. It's clear LeBron is very locked in right now. He's attacking the basket with a vengeance, getting after it defensively, moving the ball and finding the open man. He's playing like a champion.

8. Irving and Love, on the other hand, seem to be a little out of sorts. Sometimes, they're maddeningly out of sorts. Not all the time. The Cavs are still 51-21. But they're too far into the season, to close to when it really

matters, to continue losing games to crummy teams. At 20-51, the Nets are crummy.

9. Love is just too content to settle for 3-pointers. Has been all season. He was 5-of-9 inside the arc. He was 0-of-5 outside of it.

10. There's a saying in the NBA that an open shot isn't always the best shot. Sometimes you can take a dribble and move closer to the basket. Throughout history, the numbers show that shots taken further from the hoop result in a lower percentage. So sometimes, you need to have the mental fortitude to put your body on the line, drive to the hoop, and draw a hard foul.

11. The Cavs shot a total of nine free throws Thursday. So go ahead and draw your own conclusions on if they settled for too many jumpers.

12. Believe it or not, the sharpshooting Warriors are perhaps the league's best example of making the extra pass. Yes, reporters and fans love to carry on about how Steph Curry and the defending champs are a remarkable 3-point shooting team. But you don't win 64 of 71 games by standing behind the line and heaving up random shots. Instead, the Warriors share the ball, play smart, set screens and beat the defense to the hoop.

13. The Cavs are too often content to just take the first open shot. When it doesn't work — they take another. When that doesn't work, they look hopeless and helpless. Only James, it seems, attacks and tries to set up others for something near the rim.

14. I know. This is a lot of droning on about one lousy loss. And the Cavs have won 10 of 14. But in those four losses, man, the Cavs just look like an entirely different team. In those games, again, it appears they have no backup plan for when the ball doesn't drop.

15. And don't even get me started on the defense.

16. Since the coaching change from David Blatt to Tyronn Lue, the biggest positive is that most guys seem to truly enjoy playing again. That does indeed count for something, and it counts for even more against the toughest of opponents.

17. But the biggest negative has been the defense. And not doing it well for 48 minutes can crush you in the postseason.

18. Anyway, back to Irving and Love. Irving was a miserable 6-of-22 from the floor for 13 points. Why was he taking more shots than the guy who's won four MVPs and two rings? Especially when LeBron made his first 13? How does that happen? Who's to blame? I'm sorry to say I have no clue, and no one would believe me if I did.

19. Love actually grabbed 12 rebounds to go with his 11 points, so at least he contributed on the boards. But neither Love nor Irving displayed what I would call "mental toughness" for much of the night.

20. The Cavs needed both of those players — desperately. The Cavs are begging for them to play like stars. That doesn't mean exciting dribbling exhibitions or uncanny perimeter shooting. It means sacrificing your body, chasing down loose balls, keeping the ball moving, leading by example and adopting a championship mentality.

21. I've written too much already — and it's probably starting to sound like the situation is dire. It's not. But losses like this tell us the Cavs still aren't everything they believe they can be.

22. A couple of stinkers every now and then are OK. After that, it's time to look yourself in the mirror, and perhaps look your best player in the eye, and ask, "What more can I do?" Then listen, learn, and carry it with you on the court.

23. With three weeks remaining in the regular season, that may be something Irving and Love want to consider. The Cavs need them to be consistently better, and they needed it yesterday. They surely can't afford to wait another couple months.

MARCH 29

Kyrie, Cavs' D could use pick-me-up

Quick random dribbles on the Cavaliers entering Tuesday's game vs. the Rockets.

1. LeBron James will sit out to rest. I hate the idea of "rest." Not saying the Cavs are wrong or I'm right or the world should stop spinning on its axis because I have a different view. But I followed the NBA back when teams didn't have their own jets and players weren't offered sushi after every game. Why would today's players need time off?

2. LeBron or no, the Cavs must defend better as the playoffs near. They say they know that — and they did indeed do a better job Saturday vs. the Knicks. Then again, it was the Knicks, so there's no telling if any real improvement was made. Still, as long as the Cavs stick to the schemes and give proper effort, they'll be just fine. They defended well in the postseason last year and the same cast is back.

3. The only way any opponent will derail the Warriors or Spurs (or get to the Finals) is with defense. The Cavs have the offensive firepower to outscore either of those teams — really, they do. It's just that LeBron, Kyrie Irving and Kevin Love haven't been able to put it together on offense this season. At least, not as much as they should.

4. Terry Pluto pointed out this very concept in a video/blog post on cleveland.com. Pluto is a general sports columnist who covers an array of sports — but to me, remains pro basketball's most insightful writer.

5. I want to see more from Love and Irving on the floor together. So as much as I whine about it, having LeBron sit another game isn't necessarily terrible. LeBron doesn't need to get it together on a regular basis. The other two do.

6. I'm beginning to question whether Irving is the right fit at point guard for this team. Last season, I thought the guy was remarkable and the Big Three were going places. This year, I feel as if the other Big Two need Kyrie to get things figured out, share the ball, and not worry about trying to take over. This has not been a banner year for Kyrie, but there's still time to get it right.

7. If you think the Cavs are sometimes troubled, just wait until you get a load of the Rockets. Despite having tons of talent and size, Dwight Howard has proven not to be a champion — a man who suffers from chronic dissatisfaction and is always on the lookout for his next team. James Harden puts up great numbers, but apparently, those numbers mean little when it comes to winning and losing.

MARCH 30

Randomly firing away won't solve Cavs' issues

Random dribbles on the Cavaliers' awful 106-100 loss to the visiting Rockets on Tuesday.

1. This one stings. LeBron James or not, you just can't lose games where you lead by 20 points. Especially when those games are at home. Especially when it's this late in the season. Especially when this team is supposed to be more than just LeBron.

2. The Cavs lost their energy. They went away from what worked. In the first half, they played a mostly inside-out brand of basketball. At the very least, they tried to attack the rim. In the second half, they launched jumper after jumper after thankless jumper — again.

3. The Cavs have shot horribly in the fourth quarter for a week. Yet they refuse to pass the ball to Kevin Love near the basket. In fact, against the Rockets, they refused to get the ball to Love, period — as he had just one field-goal attempt the final 12 minutes.

4. This is all a broken record for a team that's 52-22 and is still in first place in the East. The Cavs don't need to be better than that, record-wise. But they do need to clean up the issues that keep playing over and over again.

5. Quick summary: The Cavs say they know what they're doing wrong, and continue to do it anyway.

6. One clear concern is the Cavs are not being nearly physical enough. They're not trying to punish teams in the paint — on either end. Instead, they're passing the ball around the perimeter and waiting for open jumpers that rarely come. On Tuesday, they shot a whopping 40 3-pointers. That's not a winning formula.

7. As Love told reporters, the Cavs just quit being aggressive in the second half. "That's ultimately what did it," he said.

8. Kyrie Irving (31 points, eight assists) knocked down a big three with 1:29 left that cut the Rockets' lead to one. But overall, Irving and Love (13 points, 11 rebounds) are still struggling to knock down dagger perimeter shots. They both missed open jumpers with about 6:00 left and the Cavs

desperately needing a score.

9. Aside from James and older players such as Richard Jefferson, James Jones, Mo Williams and Channing Frye, the Cavs too often resemble a young team that often buckles in tense situations. That's not an excuse. It's just proving to be reality.

10. And who can explain why coach Ty Lue didn't play Jones (10 points) or Williams (six points on 2-of-2 shooting) in the second half? Both performed like savvy veterans and gave the Cavs a real lift in the first.

11. This one looked a lot like the last Cavs' home game without LeBron. The Cavs blew a 20-point lead (to the Mavericks) then, too — but managed to escape with a one-point win.

12. Tristan Thompson had a nice overall night with 16 points and 10 boards. He's one guy who can never be accused of failing to give maximum effort. Thompson also broke Jim Chones' consecutive games record with the Cavs — as Thompson played in his 362nd straight.

13. Other than that, the night was a disappointment. The Cavs contained James Harden and the Rockets for the majority of three quarters, then slowly but surely let it slip away. The worst thing about it was the Cavs were so impressive in the first half — only to let it go to waste against an opponent that, frankly, hasn't displayed much resolve this season.

14. Finally, what on earth has happened to Frye? He's 4-of-22 shooting over the past four games. That includes 1-of-17 on 3-pointers. J.R. Smith (1-of-6) and Iman Shumpert (4-of-14) didn't help matters Tuesday. Shumpert, too, has been out of sorts all year.

15. The Cavs need someone, anyone, to knock down a perimeter shot. Otherwise, for the love of Dr. James Naismith, stop firing up 40 threes.

9 FINE TUNING

APRIL 1

With reasons to erupt, Cavs delivered

CLEVELAND – Random dribbles from the Cavaliers' 107-87 win over the visiting Nets on Thursday.

1. The Cavs needed a game like this. Boy, did they need a game like this. It's not often you say that about a 53-22 team. But in the Cavs' case, it's true.

2. Granted, the Nets aren't much of a test. But remember, the Cavs lost to this very team in Brooklyn just last week. OK, it wasn't exactly this team — as the Nets were without injured starting center Brook Lopez on Thursday.

3. Anyway, forget all that. The Cavs could have played the D-League Dumpster Fires and it wouldn't have mattered. After blowing a 20-point lead to the Rockets two nights earlier, the Cavs just needed to thump an opponent. They needed a fourth quarter that was little more than 12 minutes of garbage time. And they need a reminder that energy and ball movement are truly effective. On Thursday, they played the right way and made it happen.

4. LeBron James returned after a game of rest to score 24 points (on 8-of-11 shooting) in 30 minutes. He passed for 11 assists. He played with loads of energy from the start, and everyone else joined in.

5. Kevin Love also played a highly efficient game — scoring 19 points and grabbing 10 rebounds. He also went 6-of-10 from the floor and 4-of-8 on 3-pointers. Sometimes, all it takes is a late-season scrimmage such as this to rediscover your touch.

6. Even Channing Frye had a chance to find his rhythm, finishing with 13 points on 5-of-10 shooting. So overall, it was a night when few things went wrong, when the Cavs (mostly) defended, when they did the little things against a remarkably inferior opponent. That's news, as this hasn't always been the case.

7. Why just "mostly" defended? Well, Cavs coach Tyronn Lue put it this way: "I thought the first half we played great defense. In the second half we

took a step backwards, sort of messed around."

8. Still, again, the Cavs were locked in enough to do what had to be done.

9. The Big Three of James, Love and Kyrie Irving (10 points, 4-of-14 shooting) all sat the entire fourth quarter, and the Cavs once led by 32. As Jeff Kasler detailed, James, Irving and Love also had some cohesive and promising moments.

10. Yes, Irving and J.R. Smith (eight points) both struggled — but both were sick and missed the morning shootaround, and were game-time decisions.

11. Lue initially considered holding out Irving and Smith, "but they wanted to play."

12. The coach, however, did not give his star point guard a pass. "He got a lot of uncontested shots, catch-and shoot (shots)," Lue said of Irving. "He's gotta make those."

13. Lue wasn't being overly harsh or screaming Gregg Popovich-like proclamations. He's just trying to push his best players, to make everyone better as the playoffs get oh so close. And let's be honest, the Cavs could probably use some of that.

14. Despite all the negativity and drama that's been reported about this team (some true, some the laughable opposite of that) … well, guess what? With seven games left, the Cavs have equaled last season's win total.

15. Also, LeBron talked confidently about the Cavs and their prospects moving forward, in case you missed my report early Thursday.

16. So maybe the sky isn't falling, after all.

17. Irving strongly added: "Everything surrounding our team, it's just crazy to think that we're still in first place, and we're still the team to beat."

18. Still the team to beat? Believe it or not, the Cavs really believe that — and they really should. This game alone doesn't prove that. But boy, it's a start. And the Cavs needed another fresh one.

APRIL 5

Cavs sharp, so maybe rest can wait

Random dribbles on the Cavaliers' 109-80 dismantling of the host Bucks on Tuesday.

1. It's already been written 100 times I'm sure, but this is what happens when the ball moves around LeBron James. You drive, you kick, you make shots, you play off your four-time MVP.

2. On Tuesday, that was the Cavs, and they were at their finest.

3. This was little more than 48 minutes of utter garbage time, as J.R. Smith (21 points, 7-of-11 on 3-pointers) came out on fire and his teammates immediately joined the fun. This is how the Cavs should look against a young and struggling opponent.

4. In the process, Smith became the Cavs' single-season leader in threes with 197. (The previous mark of 192 was held by Wesley Person.)

5. Kevin Love scored 17 points, including 15 in the first quarter. James went for 17 points and nine assists and sat out the fourth. Kyrie Irving scored 15 and only took nine shots.

6. Imagine that. None of the Big Three hits 18 points and the Cavs win by 29.

7. I'm certainly not suggesting the Cavs make a habit of that. But it does show how well things can go when everyone is getting touches and good looks at the basket.

8. Love on the win: "We feel like we're making steps. (It's a) trust factor. Guys are stepping up, making plays, making shots."

9. Love added that the Cavs are at their best when they "respect the game." It's a phrase he seems to be turning a lot these days. "When we keep our foot on the gas pedal, we're a better team," he said.

10. The Cavs were also excellent defensively, forcing the young Bucks into silly turnovers and shots that had little hope. I feel sort of bad for the Bucks. Everyone thought they were a team on the rise — including me. But youth can be fickle, huh?

11. Speaking of D, the Cavs improved to 16-0 when holding opponents to less than 40 percent shooting.

12. If I'm Cavs coach Tyronn Lue, I'm resting LeBron, Kyrie, Love and probably even Smith for Wednesday's game at the Pacers. I mean, why not?

13. The Cavs (56-22) still lead the Raptors by 3.5 games for first in the East. I don't think there's any way they blow it. Plus, if the Pacers win, they'll increase their chances of getting the No. 7 seed. I'd rather the Pistons end up No. 8.

14. I'm not suggesting the Cavs throw the game. Nor am I insisting that resting the starters is what Lue should do. I'm just telling you what I would do. But there's a reason Lue is an NBA coach and I do ... well, whatever this is.

15. Either way, the Cavs will have a nice two-day break before visiting the Bulls on Saturday. After that, it's two home games — and then, yes, the playoffs. Hard to believe, but it's true. And the Cavs appear to be on their way to their best basketball yet.

APRIL 7

LeBron-less Cavs still lack energy

Random dribbles on the Cavaliers' 123-109 road loss to the Pacers on Wednesday.

1. The loss? Well, that's easy to understand. The Cavs played the night before (a win at Milwaukee) and LeBron James rested. The Pacers really needed a win here, too. But the manner in which the Cavs lost ... well, that's sort of getting old.

2. One bothersome thing about the Cavs is they seem to play with such little pride in games without LeBron. They don't defend, they don't play smart, and to steal a repeated phrase from Kevin Love, they don't appear to "respect the game."

3. I know Kyrie Irving (26 points, six assists) is dynamic offensively, but I wish he'd embrace more of a vocal leadership role — and make sure everyone stays engaged. Irving spends a lot of time dribbling, and yes,

scoring. Yet half the time, it's easy to wonder what he's really doing out there.

4. I don't want to sound too critical after one loss, because that's all this is. The Cavs (56-23) are still very likely to finish with the No. 1 seed in the East. And as I wrote Tuesday, they've been playing perhaps their best basketball lately. This isn't really about the big picture. It actually may be more about the past.

5. Still, if I'm Irving, I'm going into games and saying, "We don't have LeBron? No biggie. We're winning this thing." Maybe Kyrie thinks that, I don't know. If so, he's failed to deliver – as the Cavs are now 4-14 over two seasons in games without James.

6. Obviously, it's not all Irving's fault. One man rarely loses a game by himself. And Irving certainly did his part statistically. But he is supposed to be a superstar in his own right. Aren't these the times when superstars shine their brightest? When everyone thinks they have little chance?

7. Irving and Love (23 points, five rebounds) don't really work together right now — at least not when it comes to winning. I'm not sure they ever have. Both play pretty well individually with LeBron. But without him, it doesn't click and the record speaks for itself.

8. As analyst Austin Carr said on the FOX Sports Ohio postgame show, the Cavs were content to let the Pacers do what they wanted. As Cavs coach Tyronn Lue said, "Defensively, we just didn't take the challenge."

9. The Pacers (42-36) shot 56 percent from the floor, 51 percent on 3-pointers and scored 123 points. Swingman C.J. Miles torched his old team to the tune of 21 points on 7-of-9 shooting. See what I mean about lacking pride?

10. Amico Hoops columnist Jeff Kasler also touched on some of the LeBron-less Cavs issues, and I couldn't agree more with Kasler's take on Iman Shumpert. It's been a disappointing season for Shumpert after his $40-million deal in the summer. The Cavs need him to pull it together for the playoffs. And guess what? They start, like, next week.

11. No need to drone on and on or get too fired up over, again, what really was a schedule loss. But James has taken it up a notch and seems to be ready for a bigger stage. On nights like Wednesday, he probably feels all alone. He probably feels a little disheartened. The Cavs aren't supposed to

be a one-man show. But too many times minus James, that's precisely what they look like.

APRIL 9

Playoffs loom and Cavs still too clunky

Random dribbles on the Cavaliers' 105-102 road loss to the Bulls on Saturday.

1. These games barely matter, but you still would like to see someone on the Cavs (other than LeBron James) play with at least some sense of urgency.

2. Instead, everyone not named LeBron seems content to let perimeter shots determine their fate. When the jumpers don't fall, well, why bother to show any resolve or do the little things or play smart basketball? At least, that seems to be the thinking.

3. I have to keep writing, "It's just the regular season; not a big deal." But I'm tired of writing it and the readers are tired of reading it. So can we please just start the playoffs? At least then there will be no debate. Everything will be a big deal.

4. I know I'm rambling and probably not sounding real coherent. But this is what happens when the team you write about blows another big lead, looks bad in the fourth quarter, and fails to officially secure the top spot in the East – again.

5. The Bulls are basically toast. They have to win every game and hope the Pacers lose. They know the odds are against them. They were mostly out there playing for the fun of it. I'm not really sure what the Cavs were doing.

6. A couple of thoughts that might not be popular entering the final two games: First, I see no difference in the Cavs since the coaching change. They're not better, they're not worse. They're the same. I guess that's OK, but …

7. Second, what in the world is going on with Kyrie Irving? If you watch the Cavs, you know what I mean. Heck, if you're Kyrie Irving, you know what I mean.

8. Irving to reporters on his play Saturday: "I was just real (lousy) with the basketball."

9. That he was. That he has been. That is getting old.

10. Irving finished with 11 points on a clunky 5-of-17 from the floor. What has happened to his handle? What has happened to his shot?

11. He passed for eight assists, but also committed four turnovers — some in crucial moments. He's dribbling way too much, not shooting nearly well enough and barely contributing (if at all) on defense.

12. Basically, it's hard to tell if Irving is actually helping or hurting the team. I'm not trying to bash the guy. I never want to come off as overly harsh. But he doesn't look the same. And the playoffs are a week away.

13. LeBron erupted for 33 points on 13-of-17 shooting. He was again remarkable. Kevin Love went for 20 and 13 rebounds. J.R. Smith scored 24 on 8-of-16 shooting, including 7-of-14 on 3-pointers. Tristan Thompson (eight boards) hustled his buns off yet again.

14. So what was the problem? Well, the bench stunk. So did the defense for long stretches. Matthew Dellavedova airballed a wide-open three with time winding down. Smith had one blocked at the final buzzer — although it appeared he was fouled.

15. But foul, no foul, whatever. Just put the game away when you have the chance. The Bulls were on basketball life support. The Cavs offered some basketball CPR.

16. Love was also again mostly ineffective after the first quarter. This is a trend that happened too much under David Blatt, and it's happening too much under Tyronn Lue.

17. The Cavs (56-24) have two regular-season games left. Thank heavens. I don't know how much more their poor fans can take. Nearly every game is an emotional roller-coaster.

18. What seed the Cavs finish with, who they play in the first round … it doesn't really matter. The Cavs sure don't seem to care. Otherwise, this would be settled already. The fact it isn't can be downright maddening.

19. Their issues aren't huge. They're noticeable, but repairable. Still, LeBron

couldn't win a title by himself last season and he won't be able to do it alone this year. The other Cavs had better realize that soon and then decide to do something about it.

APRIL 11

Cavs clinch with cinch of a win

CLEVELAND — Love or hate how this season has unfolded for the Cavaliers, they are the No. 1 team in the East.

That is now officially official.

Kyrie Irving got his groove back, scoring 35 points, and LeBron James went for 34 in three quarters, and the Cavaliers rolled the visiting Hawks by a 109-94 count Monday.

Game, set, home-court advantage in at least the Eastern Conference portion of the playoffs.

James, Irving and perhaps several others are now likely to rest in Wednesday's regular-season finale vs. the Pistons. It probably wouldn't be a bad idea, as the Cavs (57-24) will be playing for nothing.

Then, the game after that, they begin their quest for everything.

The NBA playoffs tip off Saturday — although it won't be known until late Wednesday when the Cavs open. Cleveland's indoor football team has a game scheduled at The Q on Saturday, leading to speculation the Cavs may start Sunday.

Either way, this is a team feeling good about itself after winning a playoff-style game against a potential playoff opponent in the Hawks (48-33).

James has been absolutely on fire lately and this night was no different. He finished 13-of-16 shooting with six rebounds and six assists. He even went 3-of-4 on 3-pointers.

If James can continue to bury shots from the perimeter ... well, this can be a whole different ball game.

Kevin Love added 10 points and 14 rebounds and Matthew Dellavdova scored 10 off the bench.

The Hawks were led by Kent Bazemore and Jeff Teague, who scored 23 and 21 points, respectively. Despite the loss, the Hawks have clinched home-court advantage in the first round by virtue of the Hornets' win over the Celtics on Monday.

If there's a downside to the win, it's that only Irving and James attempted more than eight shots. The Cavs will probably need better distribution moving forward, but I have more on that in my random dribbles.

APRIL 11

For Cavs, go time is officially here

CLEVELAND – Random dribbles from the Cavaliers' convincing 109-94 victory over the visiting Hawks on Monday.

1. The real thing starts now. A regular season full of strange occurrences, occasional head scratching, and yes, plenty of wins, has basically come to a close.

2. Oh, I know. The Cavs still have a game remaining — but we won't see the regular lineup again until the playoffs. Instead, coach Tyronn Lue promised a whole lot of Sasha Kaun for Wednesday's season-finale vs. the Pistons.

3. The win Monday was mostly good. Kyrie Irving made 50 percent of his shots on his way to 35 points. LeBron James was even better, scoring 34 on a scorching 13-of-16 from the floor. He again wasn't needed in the fourth quarter.

4. Those two must score and score a lot for the Cavs to win a title. Irving will likely need shoot in the neighborhood of 50 percent on most nights. James won't necessarily need to shoot 80 percent — but it will certainly help if he can hit from the perimeter, as he has been lately and did again vs. the Hawks (3-of-4 on 3-pointers).

5. And Kevin Love (10 points, 14 rebounds) and Tristan Thompson (nine points, 10 boards) will need to rebound like madmen, and do their part to somehow protect the paint.

6. Other stuff also needs to happen, but you get the idea. I've said all year the Cavs simply must play their best basketball when it means the most. Well, it means the most now. There's no more waiting around for cohesiveness or for everything to click.

7. Lue admitted things haven't been easy since he took over for David Blatt. He credited Blatt for getting the team going early, citing the former coach's 30-11 record to start the season.

8. While the media often battled with Blatt and tended to paint a very different (and sometimes unfair) picture of Lue's predecessor, truth is, a lot

of the same trouble spots remain.

9. The Cavs (57-24) are scoring more under Lue, but some of that may have to do with James turning it up a notch (or seven). They're not as good defensively as they were earlier in the season, although they are making strides. But again, time is up. Every game means a lot after Wednesday.

10. It was good for Irving to get back into a rhythm, but he fired up 28 shots — and that's too many. LeBron took 12 less and scored just one less point.

11. This isn't intended to pit the two stars against each other. (It's not like they read my stuff anyway.) But the point is, the Cavs are going to need balance, and Kyrie is the point guard. It's up to him to direct the offense and make sure the Cavs are sharing the ball and playing the right way.

12. Frankly, I'm a little worried about that. Kyrie can be magnificent, no doubt. As I already wrote, the Cavs need him to score. But it's important not to force things. Irving is at his best when he's trying to get everyone involved early, then if that doesn't work, trying to save the day (with James) at the end.

13. Love, J.R. Smith and just about everyone else have been up and down. That's OK. It's the regular season and the Cavs still won nearly 60 games and enter the playoffs as the East's top seed. But their ultimate mission has never been to stop here. Some things still need cleaned up.

14. The Pistons could be the Cavs' first-round opponent, and Lue indicated he could throw a few different things at them Wednesday. That may even include some zone defense. Whatever it is, it's not likely to include James, Irving, Love or several others. Now until the weekend is a time for practice and rest.

15. We will know by early Thursday whether the Cavs open the playoffs Saturday or Sunday. It's all based on television. Otherwise, the NBA would have filled us in by now.

16. That's not an insult, by the way. TV pays my bills, as well as the considerably larger ones compiled by NBA franchises.

17. And here you thought this amazing website paid my bills.

18. LeBron on his remarkable play lately: "It's a mind switch. I've been

going to the gym even more, dialed in more on what needs to be done and what needs to be better."

19. I will have plenty more as the playoffs near, including series previews, what to watch, etc. Just know that what happens between now and late June will determine oh so much about this franchise moving forward.

10 THE PLAYOFFS

APRIL 16

Tristan, Cavs have board work ahead

Random dribbles on the Cavaliers, who open the playoffs Sunday afternoon at home vs. the Pistons.

1. Tristan Thompson will need to continue to keep possessions alive. That's my biggest concern if I'm the Cavs. Pistons big man Andre Drummond has been Thompson's kryptonite.

2. Cavs fans and the entire NBA know all about Thompson's value. It's primarily based on crashing the offensive glass, gathering in rebounds and kicking the ball back out to one of the big offensive weapons — LeBron James, Kyrie Irving, Kevin Love. It can be downright deflating to the opposition.

3. Thompson is best the offensive rebounder in the NBA. He may not lead the NBA in offensive rebounds. I don't know and I'm not looking it up. I don't need to. All I need is the eye test. No one demoralizes opponents with offensive rebounds like Thompson. No one.

4. And anytime I watch Thompson against Drummond ... well, Thompson isn't himself. Drummond won't allow it. Drummond is just too big. He's just too skilled a rebounder himself.

5. Thompson is 6-foot-9 and averages 9.0 rebounds a game. He wants people to believe he's 6-10, but I think even calling him 6-9 is generous. Drummond is 6-foot-11, and a lot wider. He averages 14.8 rebounds. Drummond's 16.2 points also double Thompson's scoring average (7.8).

6. This isn't to say the Thompson-Drummond matchup will determine the series. It won't. The Cavs are too talented and have too much experience. The Pistons are the future. The Cavs are the here and now.

7. But I am saying how well Thompson fares against Drummond will determine how easily the Cavs win. If Drummond does his usual number on the glass vs. Thompson, this could be a tougher series than expected for the Cavs. The Pistons are a feisty bunch and you'll need second shots

against them. Drummond virtually allows none.

8. Of course, it's not entirely on Thompson to get rebounds. Love, James, Timofey Mozgov and even the guards need to do their part. Love isn't rebounding as well this season, and he must step it up in that department. Now would be a good time to start.

9. I predict the Cavs to win in five games. I think the Pistons will steal one at home. But again, ultimately, James and the Cavs' overall experience will be too much, overwhelming even.

10. And I expect Thompson to emerge from this series as a better center than even last postseason. He won't face another big like Drummond. That much is certain.

11. LeBron on the Pistons: "They got a well-coached, balanced team and they've fought their way into the playoffs. We have to respect them."

APRIL 18

Cavs get this party started right

CLEVELAND – Random dribbles from the Cavaliers' 106-101 win over the visiting Pistons in Game 1 of the Eastern Conference playoffs Sunday.

1. I knew the Pistons wouldn't shoot 60 percent on 3-pointers all night. I knew at some point they would have to cool off. I was almost wrong.

2. Still, the Cavs trailed 83-76 in the second half and I remember thinking, "Meh. The Cavs aren't worried. They'll still probably win." They did, and that's good enough.

3. This isn't gymnastics. You don't get points for style. That's good for both teams. This was sometimes ugly. But the only thing that matters is this: Cavs 1, Pistons 0. Game 2 takes place Wednesday at The Q.

4. Kevin Love may have played his best game as a member of the Cavs. That goes beyond his 28 points and 13 rebounds. (Yes, Love compiled two more rebounds than Pistons center Andre Drummond.) It mostly has to do with the winning plays Love made all afternoon.

5. Love got switched on to fiery Pistons point guard Reggie Jackson on

three occasions — and refused to break defensively. Jackson got frustrated. He picked up a silly technical late. Love wins.

6. Love also dove to the floor in chase of a loose ball, wrestled Drummond underneath, went 4-of-8 on threes and 4-of-5 from on free throws. Love has played four playoff games for the Cavs. They may be his four best games with the team.

7. Kyrie Irving took a little longer to get going, to play the right way. He spent too much time dribbling in the first quarter — and with no real purpose. But he spent more time balancing things in the final two quarters.

8. Irving found his own shot, as well as his teammates, to help the Cavs overcome the second-half deficit. The Cavs need second-half Kyrie for the rest of the playoffs. He finished with a game-high 31 points, six assists, just one turnover and like Love, made some winning plays. The biggest from Irving may have been his blocked shot in the fourth quarter.

9. Whoever though LeBron James would be the third of the Big Three to receive mention? But in many ways, even as great as he was, James was third fiddle Sunday. Mark him down for 22 points and a whopping 11 assists, as the Cavs outscored the Pistons by 18 points with LeBron on the court.

10. One Cavs insider wondered if perhaps LeBron didn't try to take a back seat in Game 1 to get Love and Irving going, to build confidence in his younger teammates. I'm not sure I totally buy that — but it's a nice theory and may be something to consider.

11. And if so, it worked.

12. As for the negatives, the Cavs will most definitely need more from the other guys. J.R. Smith (nine points, 3-of-9 shooting) was a borderline no-show. Tristan Thompson attempted just one shot. Timofey Mozgov did the same in only five minutes. Channing Frye didn't play.

13. Then again, I thought reserves Iman Shumpert and Matthew Dellavedova did a nice job of defending the perimeter. The Pistons were just on fire, man.

14. The Pistons are feisty bunch. Beforehand, coach Stan Van Gundy tried to influence the refs by saying something about how LeBron gets all the calls. After, Jackson told reporters, "We like our chances."

15. Basically, the Pistons are pulling out all the psychological stops, and I don't blame them. They played an excellent game, and the Cavs were just so-so. Guess who won?

16. Cavs coach Tyronn Lue said part of the reason the Pistons shot so well was because his team failed to stick up a hand when closing out on shooters. Instead, the Cavs too often tried to defend with their arms at their sides. Lue was happier with the D in the second half.

APRIL 20

Cavs do what they need to do, take two

CLEVELAND – It's safe to say the Cavaliers may not have played their best playoff basketball yet.

It's safe to say it doesn't matter.

With Wednesday's 107-90 win over the visiting Pistons, the Cavs hold a 2-0 lead in the first-round series.

That's a shock to this person: Nobody.

What may be a little surprising is that the Pistons have played so hard, expended so much energy, and for the most part, looked pretty good.

And the Cavs have been less-than-perfect.

Yet here they are, a couple of wins away from advancing to the Eastern Conference semifinals.

"We wanna go into Detroit and get two more," said Cavs guard Kyrie Irving.

For the second straight game, the Cavs took flight in the second half. Irving was a big part of that, scoring 22 points overall and knocking down four of seven 3-pointers.

LeBron James scored a game-high 27 points on an icy 12-of-18 shooting. One of those was a monster dunk that rocked the rim, the gym, and the Pistons' confidence.

It truly was epic in a league where that word is thrown around too easily.

J.R. Smith scored 21 points, all on threes, and Kevin Love struggled — but collected 16 points and 10 rebounds anyway.

The Pistons were paced by Andre Drummond, who scored 20 points and grabbed 16 boards via brute force.

Drummond was equally, well, hostile from the free-throw line, where he finished a frightening 4-of-16.

"We had stretches in both games where their runs sort of got into our minds," said Pistons coach Stan Van Gundy. "We've only scored 80 second-half points (in the two games combined)."

Overall, the Cavs went 20-of-38 on threes — and as Van Gundy noted, that's darn good even if you're in a gym by yourself.

Game 3 is Friday at 7 p.m.

The Cavs will simply try to repeat what they've done each of the first two times.

"Just be ultra-aggressive and do whatever it took to win," was how Irving recapped Game 2.

APRIL 23

For Cavs, good things come in threes

Random dribbles on the Cavaliers' 101-91 win over the host Pistons in Game 3 of their first-round playoff series Friday.

1. The Cavs needed a game like that. Kyrie Irving (26 points) really needed a game like that, a shot like that. This wasn't just another win for Irving and the Cavs. Finally, they looked like the team so many think they can be.

2. Irving gave his best performance of the season. It came on the Cavs' biggest stage, in a building that was clearly against them, against an opponent that truly believed it had a chance.

3. A lot of people figured the Cavs would lose. I know I sure felt an off night coming. The Cavs won the first two games at home, but the Pistons hung with them each time. The Cavs were also sort of hit-or-miss during the regular season. This just felt like a game they would miss.

4. Clearly, they are approaching the playoffs with a different mindset. They are utilizing their Big Three of Irving, LeBron James (20 points, 13 rebounds) and Kevin Love (20 and 12) like few times before. In fact, those three have played their best three games of the year, as a unit, in the three playoff games.

5. And guess what? The Cavs lead the series, 3-0. Coincidence? Oh, you'd better believe it is not.

6. Cavs coach Tyronn Lue: "It's been the best I've seen them play, all three together."

7. Yes, I understand the Cavs are the No. 1 seed in the East — and the

Pistons are eighth. So the Cavs should advance to the next round. And yes, I understand there is still work to do. But hey, what a start to the postseason.

8. Along with the Big Three, Matthew Dellavedova was again brilliant with 12 big points (on 4-of-5 shooting) off the bench. J.R. Smith only had nine, but the Cavs outscored the Pistons by 15 with Smith on the floor. And Tristan Thompson (eight points, 10 boards) played his best game of the series.

9. So why was I worried about the Cavs entering Game 3? Because the Pistons were sort of pushing them around — and proudly pounding on their chests. The Cavs didn't really respond to the physical nature of things. They just tried to beat the young, brash wannabe Bad Boys with basketball.

10. I kind of suspected the Pistons might take the Cavs' minds off the game. At least, that seemed to be the goal of rookie Stanley Johnson, center Andre Drummond and a few others in the first two games. I admire the Pistons and their coach, Stan Van Gundy. They aren't backing down. They're showing tons of fight. And I had no idea how the Cavs would answer.

11. Well, answer they did — and then some. They acted like the favored team that they are. They conducted themselves like pros, like veterans who wouldn't be intimidated by the Pistons' attempts at basketball bullying. They looked a close game in the eye, then delivered in the clutch.

12. Nothing exemplified that more, of course, than the huge 3-pointer by Irving with 0.7 left on the shot clock and the Cavs up 95-90. By now, you know the shot about which I speak. But watch it again and again here anyway.

13. Game 4 is also at Detroit. The Cavs can close the series Sunday and give themselves a week (or more) of rest, as the Celtics and Hawks continue to beat on each other. Entering the playoffs, I wasn't sure if the Cavs had a sweep in them. I have no doubt they do now.

14. LeBron on the state of things: "I think right now we're in a great flow as far as us three. When we're on the floor we understand what we want individually and as a team. Guys are picking their spots."

APRIL 25

Look out, Cavs finding their stride

Random dribbles after the Cavaliers' 100-98 win over the host Pistons in Game 4 of their first-round playoff series Sunday.

1. It's over. I remember writing that after Game 1. But now it's official.

2. The Pistons' young, brash bunch were no match for the experience of LeBron James and friends. That group, of course, includes Kyrie Irving and Kevin Love. And watch out, NBA. The Big Three are suddenly clicking.

3. After an up-and-down regular season, Irving has saved his best for the playoffs. He scored 31 points Sunday and averaged a team-high 27.5 for the playoffs. He's hit a couple amazing shots. He's playing with great confidence.

4. Kyrie on returning from knee surgery, and the playoffs: "I knew that the preparation was for the postseason. I knew that during the regular season, there was going to be peaks and valleys, and I really just had to come to grips with it."

5. Irving still occasionally dribbles with no real purpose and messes around with the ball too much. It was a problem during the regular season. He's been better lately, though. At least now it only seems to happen in spurts.

6. Translation: Given all the great things Irving has done this postseason, the Cavs can live with him sometimes reverting to bad habits.

7. Before any of you insist Kyrie or Love or even LeBron change their ways, allow me to break out a line from the great Gregg Popovich when talking about NBA players: "He am what he am."

8. In other words, there's no such thing as the perfect player. Everyone has their flaws. Question is, can you win a title with those flaws? In the case of Irving and Cavs, I'm starting to believe, yes, you can.

9. Anyway, back to the matter at hand. James scored 22 points and grabbed 11 rebounds in the clincher. Love went for 11 and 13, respectively. But Love really struggled to shoot the ball, finishing 3-of-15.

10. Love could certainly afford to become more of an "overcomer" when

the ball isn't dropping. He seems to settle way too much. But for more on that, I'll refer you to Jeff Kasler's column on this very site.

11. Overall, I like what I've seen from the Cavs. J.R. Smith (15 points, 5-of-7 on threes) buried some truly remarkable shots. Matthew Dellavedova (11 points) and Tristan Thompson are bringing great energy.

12. My concern would be everyone off the bench not nicknamed Delly. But more on that as we move closer to the second round.

13. The Cavs await the winner of the Celtics-Hawks series that's currently tied at 2-all. That means the Cavs are off until at least Saturday — and all the way until next week if the Hawks-Celtics series goes to a Game 7. (I think it will, by the way.)

14. So the Cavs will practice and rest and aim to build on what has been a very good stretch. Not bad, huh?

· APRIL 30

LeBron: Forget Cavs' history vs. Hawks

LeBron James is 8-0 in his last two playoff series vs. the Hawks. LeBron James will tell you that means nothing.

"What happened in the past doesn't define what happens today," he said from Friday's practice.

James and the Cavaliers begin the second round of the playoffs Monday vs. the very Hawks of which James speaks. Tipoff for Game 1 is 7 p.m. at Quicken Loans Arena.

The Cavs swept the Hawks in the Eastern Conference finals last season — despite the Hawks possessing the No. 1 seed and getting the first two games at home.

This year, the Cavs own home-court advantage. Most experts predict another sweep, or the Cavs taking it in maybe five, six at most (see latest dribbles).

The Cavs also won all three regular-season meetings this year. So make it seven straight wins since the 2015 playoffs.

The numbers are clearly on the Cavs' side. So is the eye test. With James, Kyrie Irving, Kevin Love and the rest, the Cavs are just better.

The Hawks do have some talent with the likes of Al Horford, Paul Millsap and Jeff Teague. And Kent Bazemore seems to cherish the challenge of defending LeBron.

But in recent seasons, the Hawks have been the Browns to the Cavs' Steelers.

What does it all mean?

Well, again, nothing. Not if you ask LeBron.

"We've got to focus on the now and this is a (Hawks) team that's coming off a very good and challenging first-round series against the Celtics," James said. "We understand that their coach (Mike Budenholzer) is going to have those guys well-prepared and well-driven for the series."

The Hawks bounced the Celtics on Thursday, with the Cavs completing their sweep of the Pistons eight days ago.

So the Cavs appeared fairly relived to finally have a specific opponent on which they can direct their attention.

Just don't get too caught up in what's happened against that opponent in the past, James stressed.

"It don't matter if you can win 100 straight games against somebody," he said. "If you lose four in a row, then you're out of the playoffs. It doesn't matter. All the things that happened in the past do not matter to our focus this week."

MAY 3

Thompson, Cavs show right fight

CLEVELAND – Random dribbles on the Cavaliers' 104-93 roller coaster of a win over the visiting Hawks in Game 1 of the Eastern Conference semifinals Monday.

1. The Hawks went on a massive run in the second half. They still lost by double digits. What more can they possibly do?

2. That's probably the question the Hawks are asking themselves today. They played some of their best basketball of the season during about a 10-minute stretch. Yet they failed to overtake the Cavs — again.

3. For the Hawks, that's three losses in three tries during the regular season, and now five straight postseason defeats to the Cavs.

4. For the Cavs, you know all about LeBron James (25 points, nine assists) and Kyrie Irving (21 points). You know that J.R. Smith (12 points) buried an important 3-pointer late and that Kevin Love (17 points, 11 boards) again struggled shooting. But the real X-factor was Tristan Thompson.

5. Thompson just made play after play by being his usual relentless self on the offensive glass. He finished with eight points and 14 rebounds — and countless irritations of Hawks big men Al Horford and Paul Millsap.

6. Basically, even when Thompson doesn't get the rebound, he's still making life difficult for everyone else by being physical, and reaching for and slapping at the ball. It may not always lead to points for the Cavs, but it can keep the opponent from throwing a long outlet pass or getting into its offense.

7. LeBron on Thompson: "Double-T was on the glass all night. We need all the second-chance baskets and the extra possessions."

8. The Hawks are a welcome relief for Thompson. As I mentioned in the postgame podcast with Kenny Roda, Thompson no longer has to battle Pistons mammoth center Andre Drummond. The smaller Horford and Millsap must be a welcome relief.

9. Thompson on the Hawks: "Every series is different. Against the Hawks, in terms of Millsap and Horford, we are kind of the same active bigs. For me, it is just staying relentless on the glass."

10. Now, about that blown lead. ... I'd be more concerned if I thought the Hawks actually had a chance to win. At no point did I think the Cavs would lose. Maybe that's just because of the Cavs' dominance over the Hawks since LeBron returned. Maybe it's because I still feel the Hawks lack star power, or a takeover-type.

11. Hawks backup point guard Dennis Schroder (27 points) was magnificent, but nobody on the Cavs thought Schroder could beat them. They were right, as he missed some shots and made some silly mistakes at the end.

12. So what's next for the Cavs? I'd say the biggest thing is to try to get Love going. His shots are there. He's open. His teammates keep looking for him. So step up, and knock 'em down.

13. Maybe Love is thinking too much, I don't know. He seems to be at his best when he makes a few early. On Monday, he missed way too much, and occasionally seemed hesitant. Still, Love finding his range probably isn't something that's urgently necessary in this particular series.

14. And what to do about Iman Shumpert? He's been a non-factor since at least the All-Star break. Sometimes, he actually hurts the team. If he doesn't get it figured out soon, I say go with Dahntay Jones for a game and see what he's got.

15. Finally, it's still shocking to me that Timofey Mozgov has fallen so far out of the rotation. As in, Mozgov isn't in the rotation at all. I'm not saying it's the right or wrong call by coach Tyronn Lue. It's just interesting to me.

MAY 5

LeBron, Cavs deliver hammer job they wanted

CLEVELAND — Random dribbles from the Cavaliers' 123-98 blowout of the visiting Hawks in Game 2 of their second-round series Wednesday.

1. It was lots of 3-pointers (more than in any NBA game ever), excellent defense and utter domination all the way around. Think the Cavs may be coming together?

2. Most fans have been waiting for a night like this, a night when their favorite team lived up to the many expectations and just throttled somebody. This was indeed that night.

3. I thought LeBron James' comments were telling. "We had great ball movement and player movement, which we've been stressing all year," he said of the Cavs' 25 threes. "The ball finds energy and we had guys flying around offensively."

4. In other words, the Cavs did everything they set out to do when Tyronn Lue became coach. That doesn't mean fire up a bunch of threes — because they took a lot under David Blatt, too. But with Lue (and this isn't a shot at Blatt), for whatever reason, the Cavs have simply played with more passion and looked more cohesive.

5. J.R. Smith just needs to keep shooting. His 23 points and 7-of-13 on threes were really the performance of the night. And that's saying something because James scored 27. But Smith just buried some otherworldly shots. He's playing with no fear — and that's exactly what the Cavs want.

6. Smith said he can usually tell if he'll have a good shooting night when the

ball leaves his hand. Not that a night that feels "off" will keep him from shooting. And that's OK. That's why he's out there. Make or miss, the Cavs need Smith to be aggressive.

7. And as Lue said of Smith, "When he's shooting like that, it's contagious."

8. Kyrie Irving added 19 quiet points on 5-of-9 shooting, with six assists. It was another game where Kyrie forced nothing and tried to feed the open man. Like Smith, if Irving can stay within the game plan and not try to do too much, the Cavs will continue to have a shot at fantastic things.

9. Irving on the night: "Everyone was just really aggressive tonight and our decision-making was on cue."

10. Now, this was a remarkable performance by the Cavs, no doubt. But as LeBron cautioned, it doesn't matter "whether you win by 50 or 100 or one." All that matters is the Cavs lead the series, 2-0. But all they've done is take care of business at home.

11. The first game in Atlanta takes place Friday, and it's a biggie for both teams. A biggie for the Hawks because falling behind 3-0 is a basketball death sentence. And a biggie for the Cavs because following up the performance Wednesday with a clunker ... well, it would make the performance Wednesday a little less meaningful.

12. But hey, if the Cavs play like they did Wednesday, they won't have to worry about a thing. "When they put those shots down, I don't know if anyone can beat them, to be honest," said Hawks guard Kyle Korver.

13. Kevin Love had another interesting night of shooting the ball. He went 0-of-8 on twos, and 3-of-4 on threes. He also grabbed 13 rebounds as the Cavs won the war of the boards, 43-40.

14. Quick, can you name the Hawks' leading scorer? Yeah, me neither. Not without cheating and looking at the box score. (For the record, it was Paul Millsap, who had 16.) It just goes to show how well the Cavs played defensively. No member of the Hawks gave a notable performance.

MAY 9

Cavs' bright side keeps on shining

Random dribbles on the Cavaliers' 100-99 road win over the Hawks in Game 4 Sunday, completing another playoff sweep.

1. It is hard to know where to begin with the Cavaliers right now. Eight playoff games. Eight wins. Another trip to the Eastern Conference finals. And Kevin Love looks happy.

2. Actually, according to an excellent inside look at the Cavs by cleveland.com's Chris Haynes, Love *is* happy. So are the rest of the Cavs. And man, is it ever showing on the court.

3. That isn't to say things are perfect. The Cavs probably aren't where they need to be defensively. But that sure is nitpicky. For one, they're getting stops when they need 'em — Tristan Thompson's late block in Game 4 serving as just one shining example. For another, well, 8-0.

4. Love took 25 shots in 37 minutes Sunday. That was a team high. Wonder why the guy is happy? That's a joke, but there is some truth to it. The Cavs are looking for Love, and in all the right places.

5. Love finished with 27 points and 13 rebounds. LeBron James went for 21 points, 10 boards and nine assists — and forced the jump ball with 2 seconds left that basically ended the series.

6. Kyrie Irving almost seemed like a "third fiddle" again. One Twitter follower even asked, "What's wrong with Kyrie? Is he sick?" Ah, yes. The Twitter crowd. Sometimes witty and lovable, sometimes something far different than that.

7. Truth is, Irving was just fine, compiling 21 points himself. He went 8-of-16 from the floor. He passed for eight assists. He played a complete game. So what's wrong with Kyrie? Just a hunch, but I surmise not a darn thing.

8. Kyrie on the sweep: "This is more than I dreamed of. It's what I genuinely enjoy about basketball, playing with great guys."

9. LeBron on the state of the Cavs: "We're in a great rhythm right now. We know exactly where we want to be on the floor."

10. Thompson finished with 10 rebounds. Interestingly, J.R. Smith took just four shots in 36 minutes for three points. That seems a little odd, but … 8-0.

11. As for the Hawks, well, who knows what's next. This is a good team and a classy organization. You have to keep Mike Budenholzer, the coach and man in charge of the roster. But it may be time to say goodbye to Kyle Korver (next year is a contract year). Also, Al Horford and Kent Bazemore are free agents. A shakeup is likely.

12. Back to the Cavs. Iman Shumpert played his best postseason game with 10 points. He actually looked confident out there. Channing Frye followed his monster Game 3 with eight points. Shumpert and Frye were each 3-of-6 shooting.

13. The Cavs now have 11 straight wins over the Hawks, dating back to the conference finals last season. That's domination, folks.

14. Question is, will the next round be any tougher for the Cavs? They'll play either the Raptors or the Heat. Both of those teams remain fickle well into the playoffs. The Cavs, on the other hand, are clearly on solid ground.

11 EASTERN KINGS

MAY 17

Cavs need to take it up a notch vs. Raptors

Random dribbles on the Cavaliers, who begin play in the Eastern Conference finals Tuesday vs. the Raptors.

1. This one isn't likely to be as easy. Not that sweeps over the Pistons and Hawks were a stroll through hoops heaven, but as LeBron James said of the Raptors: "They're here for a reason."

2. While somewhat inconsistent when it comes to shooting the ball, the Raptors' backcourt of Kyle Lowry and DeMar DeRozan is among the league's most explosive. Those two are stars, but still may not be appreciated enough.

3. Read: Kyrie Irving, J.R. Smith and the other Cavs guards will need to be at their best.

4. The Cavs will catch a little bit of a break, as Raptors center Jonas Valanciunas is out for at least Game 1 with an ankle injury. Valanciunas is averaging 15.0 points and 12.1 rebounds in the playoffs. He's always a problem.

5. Filling in for Valanciunas is Bismack Biyombo, gifted in his own right. Biyombo is springy, athletic and plays with lots of energy — sort of like Cavs big man Tristan Thompson.

6. Biyombo is averaging 6.1 points and 8.9 rebounds in 22.7 minutes this postseason. Thompson is at 5.0 and 8.3, respectively, in 28.8 minutes.

7. Once again, the Cavs will need a big series from Kevin Love and, yes, Channing Frye off the bench. This will also be a good series for Matthew Dellavedova to get going again — as the Raptors have a good one off the bench in reserve guard Cory Joseph.

8. Meanwhile, perhaps the biggest X-factor for the Raptors is small forward DeMarre Carroll. He is also known as The Guy Who Guards LeBron.

9. Carroll did the same in the East finals last year, it was just while playing with the Hawks. He does a decent job on James, getting physical and staying in LeBron's face. LeBron will need to make some perimeter shots in this series to keep Carroll honest.

10. I suspect the Raptors to be physical and ornery all series. Toronto is close, so their fans will be in Cleveland, and acting proud and loud. Canada's first love is hockey, but the Raptors truly have one the league's best and most boisterous fan bases.

11. None of it will matter, though. Just like I've written about the Cavs' first two playoff opponents, this is a talent issue. The Cavs simply have more star power and experience than the Raptors. Cavs in five.

MAY 18

Game 1? For Cavs, nothing but fun

CLEVELAND — Random dribbles from the Cavaliers' 115-84 hammer job of the visiting Raptors in Game 1 of the Eastern Conference finals Tuesday.

1. That was easier than I expected. That was probably easier than the Cavs expected. And it was likely a whole lot worse than what the Raptors expected.

2. It was a basketball assault. The Cavs didn't need 3-pointers — they just attacked the rim, and they did so a vengeance.

3. Kyrie Irving scored 27 points on 11-of-17 shooting. LeBron James scored 24 on 11-of-13. LeBron also made his first nine shots. It was as if he was just toying with cats out there.

4. The Cavs were 7-of-20 on threes. That after a series in which they averaged 19 makes a game. So seven was a low number. But they still shot 55 percent from the floor.

5. Cavs coach Tyronn Lue on that very topic: "We always want to play inside-out ... it opens up the 3-point shot for us. We just take what the defense gives us."

6. And the bench, my goodness. The Cavs' best lineup may have been

James, Channing Frye, Matthew Dellavedova, Iman Shumpert and Richard Jefferson.

7. Actually, "best lineup" may be a stretch. But that unit really did come in and help open a major lead early in the second quarter. They created turnovers and turned them into easy buckets. That's winning basketball.

8. The Cavs also did a defensive number on Raptors star guard Kyle Lowry — who finished 4-of-14 for eight points. Lowry looked a little tired after two consecutive seven-game series. And the pace of this one seemed to get to him.

9. As Raptors coach Dwane Casey pointed out: "The speed of the game was an issue."

10. Casey went on to say the Cavs are quicker than the Heat and Pacers, the Raptors' first two postseason opponents. "We gotta make that adjustment," Casey said.

11. Lowry on Irving: "He's playing fantastic. Throughout the season, he got more comfortable coming back from the (knee) injury. He's more confident right now."

12. DeMar DeRozan led the Raptors with 18 points, and Bismack Biyombo scored 12. Other than that, it wasn't pretty — as the Raptors were a miserable 42 percent from the field and 21 percent on threes.

13. It's a little hard to believe after such a hit-or-miss regular season that the Cavs are 9-0 in the playoffs. But that's the situation right now. This is a team that has really turned it on.

14. Kevin Love, by the way, has now improved to 13-0 lifetime in the postseason. He finished with a quiet (and efficient) 14 points and four rebounds. Interestingly, Jefferson led the Cavs with 11 boards.

15. Remember, before the game, LeBron said the Cavs were "ready for whatever." He reiterated those comments after the win.

16. LeBron on adaptability: "Tonight, they wanted us to be in the paint. But as I keep telling you guys, we're not a jump shooting team. We're a balanced team. What every game dictates, we adjust to that."

MAY 22

Suddenly, a Game 4 that matters for Cavs

Random dribbles on the Cavaliers' 99-84 loss to the host Raptors in Game 3 of the Eastern Conference finals Saturday.

1. For the first time all playoffs, Kevin Love, Kyrie Irving and Tristan Thompson looked like they'd never been here before.

2. Irving tried to do too much. That's not intended to be a major criticism. But when you're 3-of-19 from the floor ... well, you may have been forcing things.

3. Irving admitted after the game he was bad. He spoke confidently about bouncing back. Let's hope he's right, because the Cavs really need Game 4 (more on that in a moment).

4. Love was horrendous. You could even live with his 1-of-9 shooting. But he just seemed timid and generally lacked toughness. It was like the guy had never played a playoff game. And remember, this is the same man who entered the night with a 14-0 lifetime record in the postseason.

5. Meanwhile, Bismack Biyombo grabbed 26 rebounds against the Cavs' frontcourt of Love and Thompson. These are max-contract guys. Biyombo makes ... what again? Oh, never mind.

6. Anyway, it's not really about the money. It's about Love and Thompson not playing with enough zeal and aggressiveness and mental toughness to offset Biyombo. The Cavs' two starting big men, along with LeBron James, should always control the boards. Instead, Love has been absent on the glass all series.

7. James played like a champion with 24 points, eight rebounds and five assists. J.R. Smith kept the Cavs within striking distance much of the night, scoring 22 points and going 7-of-16 on 3-pointers. He also grabbed five rebounds.

8. Smith's lone issue was his trying to slow DeMar DeRozan, who erupted for a game-high 32 points.

9. I'm not gonna ramble on and on about this one. The Cavs just didn't

bring it. The Raptors did. Hopefully for the Cavs' sake, they learned from it. They still lead the series, 2-1, with Game 4 Monday in Toronto.

10. LeBron on the loss: "We didn't play our game and they made us pay for it. We didn't start the game as physical as we should have at the point of attack."

11. What's so bizarre is I never expected the Raptors to find a way to solve the Cavs after the two massacres in Cleveland. But Dwane Casey is a bright coach and these Raptors have always been resilient.

12. The Cavs should do themselves a favor and come out like they mean it Monday. If not, a similar result is likely to happen. Then all of a sudden, everyone goes from talking about the 10-game winning streak to start the playoffs — to the the series being knotted, 2-2.

13. If the Cavs win Monday, they head back home up 3-1 with all the momentum and every reason to put it away. But they'll need Irving, Love and Thompson (at least), and they'll need them to be a lot more productive than Saturday night.

MAY 24

Still no time for a Cavs panic attack

Random dribbles on the Cavaliers' 105-99 loss to the host Raptors in Game 4 of the Eastern Conference finals Monday.

1. When it comes to the Cavs, this may be a little more positive than you're expecting. But I believe they're still OK. I believe this series is still their series to lose.

2. Yes, it's tied at 2-all. No, the Cavs haven't looked especially good the past two games. And my oh my, where are Kevin Love and Tristan Thompson?

3. Still, the Raptors have yet to win in Cleveland this season. The next game is in Cleveland. That doesn't mean the Cavs only need to set foot on the court. I kind of get the feeling that's what they thought before Game 3 — and man, did they ever pay.

4. But the Cavs did figure out some things in Toronto in the second half of Game 4. Namely, they learned they can get back in the game quickly when

they really move the ball, hit a couple 3-pointers and score at the rim.

5. The ball movement and shooting was mostly a thing of beauty in the fourth quarter. The defense was not. As well as the Cavs played offensively, they got zero big stops.

6. As I wrote in my instant analysis column, LeBron James played brilliantly in scoring 29 points. And Channing Frye (12 points) was fairly clutch with his 3-point shooting.

7. Kyrie Irving scored 26, but I would characterize his overall performance as just fair. He did make some gutsy shots. He again struggled defensively, though — as Raptors point guard Kyle Lowry erupted for a game-high 35.

8. Kyrie, Love, Tristan. Those three are playing like it's their first time on this stage. For Love, I guess it actually is, as a shoulder injury kept him out of the Eastern Conference finals last season.

9. Still, these guys have the benefit of playing with James. Unfortunately, none have shared his championship mentality of being better as the stakes get higher. That's really the most disappointing thing when it comes to this team. The young guys are suddenly playing like young guys.

10. All of that said, the Cavs won 57 games. The Raptors won 56. And teams such as the Raptors play much better at home than, say, the Pistons and Hawks do. So the fact this series is tied doesn't need to be a huge shock. Not even Michael Jordan and Magic Johnson swept every series. So let's be realistic.

11. A lot of folks in the social media world, as well as on TV and radio, love to talk about how much more they know than the coach. Frankly, I'm sick of reading/hearing it. I think Tyronn Lue has done a fine job. He's not a huge reason why the Cavs won and he hasn't been to blame when the Cavs lose. He's setting the players up to succeed. And several of them just didn't deliver in Toronto.

12. So what now? I still say Cavs in six. The Raptors are a tough team and they'll be back in the East finals someday, if not next year. But the Cavs played terrible for most of Game 4 and almost won. I don't think the Cavs will play this bad again.

MAY 26

Again, Cavs play like they mean it

CLEVELAND — Random dribbles from the Cavaliers' basketball bloodbath of a 116-78 win over the visiting Raptors in Game 5 of the Eastern Conference finals Wednesday.

1. That's about as easy as it gets. The Cavs did little wrong. The Raptors did nothing right. The Cavs lead, 3-2. On to Game 6, please.

2. All of the Cavs were angry. They felt they let down their guard in Toronto. They felt they should've won Game 4 — when they overcame an 18-point deficit to take a three-point lead late in the second half.

3. The Cavs had won 10 straight playoff games before visiting Toronto. Then they had to hear and read everything said about how they were dominated by the likes of Kyle Lowry and DeMar DeRozan. Heck, there was even talk Bismack Biyombo played his way into a major contract, all because of his huge games against the Cavs.

4. So the Cavs came out fiery, focused, and determined to make Kevin Love (25 points) forget those previous two miserable nights.

5. The rest was just … well, you saw it. The Raptors should've stayed home, man.

6. Mostly, the Cavs rarely settled, really defended and took the ball to the basket like they meant it.

7. Love on the win: "On the offensive end, on either a miss or a make, as long as we are getting good shots, getting to the rim and being aggressive, we are always a better team when we do that."

8. Love finished 8-of-10 shooting. LeBron James and Kyrie Irving each played an extremely efficient game all the way around, scoring 23 apiece.

9. Tristan Thompson clearly became agitated with all the questions about Biyombo during the morning shootaround. Thompson did something about it, scoring nine points and collecting 10 rebounds. He again was everywhere.

10. I thought LeBron had some interesting takes after the game. For one,

he praised Love during the interview on ESPN, saying the Cavs "followed his lead."

11. More LeBron on Love: "Tonight was just a bounce-back (game) for him."

12. Another interesting LeBron quote: "We didn't get to this point in the season by me taking over every game."

13. More LeBron: "My presence on the floor is much bigger than what the numbers talk about."

14. And Cavs fans everywhere give a hearty amen.

15. Finally, these incredibly true words, also from LeBron: "There may be a time when I may have to have one of those big games. But until then, just relax."

16. Interestingly, James now leads the Cavs in postseason scoring at 23.9 points. That's a shade better than Kyrie and his 23.8. Love is at 17.1.

17. Game 6. The Cavs should remember what happened in Game 5 and try to do it again. But as we know, the Raptors are no pushovers — especially at home. The Cavs will need to play every bit as well as they did Wednesday. They can't afford to be wimps.

18. Five more wins, and Cleveland will have its first championship since 1964.

MAY 28

This time, Cavs finish with a purpose

Random dribbles on the Cavaliers' 113-87 win over the host Raptors to clinch the Eastern Conference championship Friday.

1. When LeBron James and the Cavaliers get you figured out, you're in trouble. That's the lesson learned in the East playoffs, and particularly, the conference finals.

2. The Cavs had their way with the Raptors in the first two games. The next two games were the exact opposite of that — as the Cavs suddenly turned

to mush. The Raptors undoubtedly had something to with that.

3. Then came Games 5 and 6. The Cavs blitzed Raptors guards Kyle Lowry and DeMar DeRozan. Those two also happen to be the Raptors' best players and biggest threats. When the Raptors win, it's because Lowry and DeRozan are getting free and going nuts.

4. The Cavs contained the Raptors' brightest stars in the final two games of the series — and it was blowout city. So as good as the offense has been in these playoffs (and it's been outstanding for all but two games), Tyronn Lue finally has his troops figuring out things on defense. That should bode well moving forward.

5. I'm not writing too much about Game 6. I was impressed with how the Cavs never let the Raptors feel comfortable, and how James (33 points, 11 rebounds), Kyrie Irving (30 points, nine assists) and Kevin Love (20 points, 12 boards) gave the Cavs everything they needed from the Big Three. That's how stars on championship teams perform — especially in big road games.

6. Irving told FOX Sports Ohio: "We're not satisfied."

7. Both Kyrie and LeBron were emotional in postgame interviews with sideline reporters. Not sure why, but this year's Cavs run seems more special to the players. They are definitely more united under Lue.

8. Of course, they are also healthier. This will be the first Finals appearance for Love.

9. Lue on the idea of a title: "This city has been craving a championship. We have the right team and we have the right talent."

10. LeBron on the same topic: "I know our city deserves it, our fans deserve it. But that gives us no sense of entitlement. We've still got to go out and get it. We've still got to go out and prove ourselves."

11. If I'm the Cavs, I honestly can't say who I'd rather face — the Warriors or the Thunder. Both teams present an array of problems.

12. If I absolutely, positively had to choose, it would be the Thunder, but only because the Cavs would own home-court advantage. Then again, do you really want to see Kevin Durant and Russell Westbrook instead of another team? Man, I do not know.

13. Regardless, the Cavs have to win four more games before their next opponent wins three. I think they can do it against anyone. I really do.

12 MODERN MIRACLE

JUNE 2

Underdog? Cavs are it, or so they say

Random dribbles on the Cavaliers, who begin their Finals rematch with the Warriors on Thursday.

1. Whoever thought a team with LeBron James would be considered David to someone else's Goliath?

2. Actually, that would be understandable in the early years of James' career. The Cavs were heavy underdogs to the Spurs in the Finals of 2007 — and rightfully so. But now? James is a two-time champion, a four-time MVP, and has Kyrie Irving and Kevin Love beside him.

3. Still, the Cavs are the underdogs. Not necessarily according to me, but clearly according to the rest of the basketball-loving universe. (Oh, and the oddsmakers.)

4. Now, again, it may be understandable. Steph Curry, Klay Thompson and the Warriors have been riding their magical basketball train for nearly two years. They defend, they make shots, they play together, they play like champions. They won 73 doggone games, man.

5. The Cavs? Well, they've looked excellent for 11 and a half games of the postseason. For the other game and a half, they stunk. Their playoff record is 12-2. The Warriors are 12-5. The Cavs have been a better playoff team. But yes, I consider the competition.

6. Honestly, I don't get too bothered by any of it. These teams just need a game. LeBron and the Cavs have pressure — because they're supposed to be better this time around, with a healthy Irving and Love. The Warriors have pressure, too — because not winning a title will make their 73-9 season seem pointless.

7. Granted, none of this is actually true. Nobody here is a big loser. But only one team can win. Whoever doesn't will almost certainly have an excellent shot to do it again next season.

8. Of course, nothing is a given. People get injured. Teams can suddenly forget how to be cohesive. The grind of the season can wear on even the brightest of stars. So it's best to try to focus on the present and try to win it all now.

9. Either way, I know you're all nervous. I don't blame you. You think about losing again to the Warriors — and it's anxiety city. Or if you're a Warriors fan (and I know some of you read, and I am grateful for it), you think about 73-9 potentially going to waste — and it's anxiety city for you, too.

10. Bottom line? Well, as LeBron said, "Underdog, overdog … it's all stupidity." And he's right. Regardless of what you read, hear or watch on TV, nothing is settled until one team wins four more. So try to just enjoy the ride. And oh, save me a seat in anxiety city. I'll be right there with you.

JUNE 3

Cavs check reserve, come up empty

The Cavaliers held a one-point lead with just about 2:00 left in the third quarter and the Warriors' top two guys had done next to nothing.

Then somehow, the Cavs managed to do nothing but sputter themselves for the remainder of Game 1 of the Finals.

The result was a 104-89 road loss to defending champions, with the final moments turning into little more than garbage time.

How did it happen?

Well, for starters, it was actually the bench — and not the starters.

While the Cavs did a defensive number on Warriors stars Steph Curry (11 points, 4-of-15 shooting) and Klay Thompson (nine points, 4-of-12 shooting), they couldn't seem to contain anyone else.

Shaun Livingston came off the bench to become the player of the game, scoring 20 points on a sizzling 8-of-10 from the floor.

Leandro Barbosa finished with 11 points on 5-of-5. And Andre Iguodala, last year's Finals MVP, scored 12 biggies and was a plus-22.

These are players who were supposed to be done four years ago. But they benefit from a system that focuses on teamwork, smart passes and good shots.

Overall, the Warriors' reserves outscored the Cavs' by a 45-10 count.

Forty-five … to 10.

As for the stars, Kyrie Irving went for 26 points and tried mightily (perhaps sometimes too mightily) to bring the Cavs back.

LeBron James finished with 23 points, 12 rebounds and nine assists, and Kevin Love went for 17 points and 13 boards.

Other than that, the Cavs got nothing.

J.R. Smith, for instance, took three shots, scored three points and while he did a decent job on Thompson, was a non-factor.

The Warriors' 7-0 run to close the third quarter carried over to the fourth — where it swelled to 15-0 and 33-12, and the Warriors dominated the rest of the way.

"We took LeBron out at the end of the third quarter, and the game kind of got away from us," Cavs coach Tyronn Lue said.

Love added to reporters in Oakland: "That was the point where we really needed to take (control), but you gotta hand it to them, they played a hell of a game."

The Cavs finished 7-of-21 on 3-pointers, compared to 9-of-27 for the Warriors.

JUNE 3

Cavs must find more go for the O

Random dribbles on the Cavaliers' 104-89 loss to the host Warriors in Game 1 of the Finals on Thursday.

1. It's too bad the Cavs have to wait until Sunday for the next game. They want another crack at the Warriors, like, now.

2. LeBron James: "Two days between (games) doesn't help, doesn't feel good."

3. In other words, the Cavs could have played much better and they know it. It's pretty evident they feel like they did more wrong than the Warriors did right. The Cavs get at least three more chances to prove it.

4. I'm not here to tell you everything is great. For the Cavs, it's not. But it's not panic time. It's not panic time until you lose on your own floor. And it's not panic time until the likes of Warriors subs Shaun Livingston (20 points) and Leandro Barbosa (5-of-5 shooting) prove they can have another game like this.

5. I know, I know. Steph Curry (11 points) and Klay Thompson (nine) were useless — and the Warriors still ran away with it. But defensively, I was OK with the Cavs' game plan. They dared the Warriors' role players to beat

them, and the Warriors' role players did. Can those role players do it in Cleveland? I say no. I have my doubts they can even do it in Game 2 on Sunday.

6. And what choice do the Cavs have? In Game 1, they had to pick their poison. Given the circumstances, I'd give Livingston better looks at the basket than Curry and Thompson every day of the week and twice on Sunday.

7. A bigger issue was the Cavs' offense. Yes, Kyrie Irving scored 26 points. Yes, James neared a triple-double with 23 points, 12 rebounds and nine assists. And yes, Kevin Love was solid with 17 points and 13 boards. But the offense was still too stagnant, as no one else really got involved.

8. More LeBron: "Defensively, we followed the game plan as much as possible. Offensively, we gotta be much better moving the ball, moving bodies."

9. The Cavs trailed the series to these same Warriors by the same 1-0 count last season. They tied the series at 1-all heading back to Cleveland. Most Cavs fans would take that again this year. And guess what? That's still possible.

10. Kyrie Irving: "We just gotta keep playing and remain calm."

11. That's not earth-shattering analysis, but the Cavs have it right. They can't get too freaked out, and as LeBron suggested, they must do a better job of mimicking the Warriors — by taking care of the ball, making the smart play and finishing at the rim.

12. The Warriors are a great team, a team that finished 73-9. You have little margin for error and you'll likely need help from an unexpected source or two (Earth to J.R. Smith and Channing Frye).

13. But the Cavs are pretty good, too. They still believe they can win this. Until they lose four, it's the best way to approach things. Right? Right. "We'll figure it out for Game 2," Tristan Thompson said.

JUNE 5

Can Cavs match Warriors ways?

1. If you had told me two years ago that a team whose three main weapons were Shaun Livingston, Leandro Barbosa and Andre Iguodala would beat a team whose three main weapons were LeBron James, Kyrie Irving and Kevin Love, I would've laughed you out of the gym.

2. But that's what happened in Game 1.

3. That's one reason I'm concerned about the Cavaliers and their 1-0 deficit. I can't help but wonder if the Warriors are just in their heads.

4. I also fear the Warriors are a bad matchup for the Cavs. Granted, at 73-9, the Warriors are a bad matchup for a lot of teams. But remember when the Cavs compiled 66 wins in 2009 and lost to the Magic in the East playoffs? It's because the Cavs couldn't beat a "system" team that was in rhythm.

5. That said, I'm not ready to write off the Cavs. I won't even say Game 2 is a "must-win." I mean, if the Cavs go down 2-0 … then win both their home games … I think everybody in Cleveland will be feeling pretty good again.

6. Anyway, back to the Warriors.

7. Remember how everyone said you needed a "super team" to win titles? Or maybe they called it "super friends," I'm not really sure. I just know there sure are a lot of baffoons in the media — because the Warriors are everything you were told a team couldn't be.

8. Steph Curry was drafted seventh overall out of Davidson. Klay Thompson was chosen 11th overall out of Washington State. Draymond Green was selected 35th, a second-rounder.

9. And while Andrew Bogut was a No. 1 overall pick, no one exactly had high expectations of him when he was traded from the Bucks (with Stephen Jackson) to the Warriors — for Kwame Brown, Monta Ellis and Ekpe Udoh.

10. Yeah, I totally forgot about Kwame, too.

11. And then there are the likes of Livingston, Barbosa and Iguodala,

players who weren't known for winning big games or hitting their big shots. All were considered over-the-hill prior to the start of last season.

12. Also, Steve Kerr is in just his second season as a coach — at any level. At this rate, he'll be right up there with Red Auerbach, Gregg Popovich and Phil Jackson.

13. So what's my point: Well, it's that the Warriors are proof that getting a super-duper star from another team isn't necessary. Instead, you can be a success by making the most of your draft picks and building a winning culture.

14. Read: Kevin Durant isn't signing with the Warriors because the Warriors don't need him. They won't be spending a ton of money and creating cap space for a guy who they repeatedly beat.

15. As for the Cavs, most people I've spoken with from around the league aren't real high on their chances. Frankly, while I hope those people are wrong, I don't blame them. The Cavs have not shown they know how to close games against this particular team.

16. Game 2 would be a good place to start. It's where the Cavs' Big Three can show the world they're not done yet. But to win this series, I'm afraid coach Tyronn Lue and the Cavs will have to come up with a little bit of magic. The kind of magic, no doubt, that the Warriors have been riding.

JUNE 6

Right now, Cavs in a world of hurt

Random dribbles on the Cavaliers' embarrassment of a 110-77 loss to the host Warriors in Game 2 of the Finals.

1. Well, at least the series shifts to Cleveland now. Don't know about you, but if I'm rooting for the Cavs, that's about all I can come up with.

2. Seriously, though. If the Cavs hope to overcome their 2-0 deficit, they'd better man up. It's time to put on your big boy pants, it's time to quit being so soft, it's time to stop letting the Warriors push you around and clap in your face.

3. Even Cavs coach Tyronn Lue said it: "We've got to be tougher."

4. LeBron James had a near triple-double (19 points, nine assists, eight rebounds), but that doesn't mean he was good. At least, he was not good for a guy who's supposed to be leading the way.

5. James committed seven turnovers, too often looked lost on defense and couldn't muster a single point in the first quarter.

6. That's not to question LeBron's overall greatness. But he's been to six straight Finals and it's up to him to set the winning example on the court. He failed to be that leader in Game 2.

7. That said, LeBron cannot be expected to carry a team to a title by himself. As sad as it is to admit, he just may not be that guy anymore. Plus, he's getting zero help.

8. Kyrie Irving (10 points) and Kevin Love (five before leaving with a head injury) were supposed to be the younger stars who made winning a championship easier this time around. Oftentimes, though, their inexperience on this stage really shows.

9. Unless the Cavs pull off the biggest shocker in Finals history and come back to win this thing, it may be time to put an end to the current version of the Big Three. So far, it's fizzled.

10. But that's talk for another day. Right now, the Cavs have to figure out a way to get involved in this series and give themselves a fighting chance. Don't ask, though. I have no idea how.

11. But I would've said the same thing about the Raptors when they were down 2-0 to the Cavs. I saw no reason for hope. But then they went to Toronto and whipped the Cavs twice. If the Cavs can do the same, and tie the series at 2-all … well, let's just wait and see.

12. The Warriors have totally shut down the Cavs from the perimeter. Actually, the Warriors held the Cavs to just 35 percent shooting overall in Game 2.

13. But the Cavs were just 5-of-23 on 3-pointers — including a 3-of-16 brickfest by the starters. Former coach and current analyst Hubie Brown called the Cavs' inability to repeat their early playoff marksmanship the "biggest upset of the Finals."

14. Love is going through the NBA's concussion protocol and may not be available for Game 3 Wednesday at The Q. If he can't play, Lue can either go smaller and start Richard Jefferson or go bigger with Channing Frye — who's been MIA in the first two games. Jefferson has actually done some nice things.

15. I could ramble on and on about Game 2, but what's the point? This series starts Wednesday. That has to be the Cavs' approach — and they'd better pull it together, toughen up and make it clear to the Warriors that this will no longer be easy.

JUNE 8

Cavs must find way to fix this basketball pain

CLEVELAND — Random dribbles on the Cavaliers entering Game 3 of the Finals vs. the Warriors on Wednesday.

1. This has been a basketball nightmare for the Cavs on the NBA's biggest stage. I wish I had some sort of solution. I don't.

2. I've been reading a lot about what the Cavs need to do. I've seen writers offer opinions on how to slow down the Warriors — and that's OK. That's what writers and analysts (such as Yours Truly) are paid to do. But I'm not sure I can believe any of it.

3. I hate to sound like a Negative Nancy here. I'm just being honest. I've seen little reason for the Cavs to have hope after the first two games. The Warriors have dominated in every facet — scoring, defense, bench, you name it. It hasn't been close.

4. LeBron James called Game 3 a must-win, and man, he's right about that one. He can't get ahead of himself, but the Cavs must win the next two. If they can do that, then they may have solved the Warriors, and it's a series. But as the great ones say over and over, let's just take care of Game 3 first.

5. I spoke with several opposing executives and scouts who offered suggestions for the Cavs. I'll be sharing those before Game 3 on the FOX Sports Ohio pregame show. Cavaliers Live starts at 7:30 p.m.

6. J.R. Smith, Channing Frye, Matthew Dellavedova and Iman Shumpert have been no-shows for the Cavs. That really hurts, because those guys

played such valuable roles in getting this far. Well, at least Smith and Frye have.

7. Meanwhile, Delly and Shumpert have looked lost for most of the season. Both were so valuable during last season's playoff run — but right now, they appear as if this is their first Finals.

8. Finally, nobody really asked, but I believe they need to get more physical. The Warriors aren't afraid of contact, but the Cavs haven't even begun to test that theory. They've been much too soft. Maybe that will change with the home fans behind them.

JUNE 9

Finally, Cavs show championship drive

CLEVELAND — Random dribbles from the Cavaliers' convincing 120-90 win over the visiting Warriors in Game 3 of the Finals on Wednesday.

1. When the Cavaliers play like this — physical, aggressive, attacking — they give themselves a chance in this series. All that matters right now is they do it again Friday night.

2. Or as coach Tyronn Lue said: "We know Friday we have to play even better. I think we're ready for that."

3. Lue is right. The Warriors are gonna be ticked. They stunk in Game 3. The Cavs had something to do with that, maybe a lot to do with that. But the Warriors have been the ultimate bounce-back team.

4. Jumping out to 9-0 lead set the tone for the night. Kyrie Irving (30 points, eight assists) was magnificent early. LeBron James (32 points, 11 rebounds) found his jumper late. It was a lethal all-around night from the Cavs' brightest stars.

5. LeBron on his performance: "My teammates told me to be aggressive. That's what I was."

6. Perhaps more than that, the Cavs received strong performances from J.R. Smith (20 points, 5-of-10 on 3-pointers) and Tristan Thompson (14 points, 11 boards). Neither played well on the road. But man, they sure came to life at The Q.

7. I suspect that's what this series will be about — the guys who aren't considered "stars." And if the Cavs are to have a chance, they'll need the Smiths and Thompsons of the roster to flourish.

8. Richard Jefferson started in place of Kevin Love (concussion), and Jefferson's contribution went beyond his nine points and eight underrated rebounds. He also helped lead the charge when the idea was defense and being physical.

9. It was that mindset from Jefferson and all the Cavs that again kept Warriors standouts Steph Curry (19 points) and Klay Thompson (10) from going bananas. The Splash Brothers finished just 10-of-26 shooting.

10. I'm sure there have already been 2,976 opinions written about Love and what the Cavs should do with him for Game 4. My opinion? Well, I'm with Warriors coach Steve Kerr, who suggested the outcome would've been the same had Love played.

11. That said, I'd still bring Love off the bench on Friday (assuming he's fully recovered). Jefferson has looked good in the Finals. He may be a better matchup vs. the Warriors' starters. And perhaps Love could have success against the Warriors' reserves.

12. But again, such a move wouldn't be to punish Love. It'd be to reward Jefferson, and hey, it sure worked in Game 3.

13. Anyway, we'll know a lot more about what both teams will actually do between now and tipoff Friday. The Cavs should simply aim for more of the same. Energy, aggressiveness, physicality. All three worked well in Game 3. But you need all three.

14. Kerr on the night: "We weren't ready to play. They punched us in the mouth right away. ... It's the NBA. That's just how it is."

JUNE 9

Cavs have tough call on Love

CLEVELAND – Much is being made of Kevin Love's absence, and the Cavaliers' easy win, in Game 3 of the Finals.

The two things may or may not be related. Frankly, I'm not really sure.

I think the Cavs and their fans are just happy to get a convincing victory again. I think the Cavs and their fans now only care about getting another one Friday — which would tie their series vs. the Warriors at 2-all.

And just being at Quicken Loans Arena again may have been enough.

But yes, it's fair to ask if the Cavs won by 30 because they match up better without Love, who rested with a concussion.

Or maybe the question isn't whether the Cavs match up better minus Love altogether, but simply without Love as a starter.

Maybe Richard Jefferson is just a better fit as the starter in this particular series. Maybe Love would be best used, and more productive, if coach Tyronn Lue brought him off the bench.

I'm not trying to provide concrete answers here. I'm mostly just thinking out loud.

And I do mostly agree with Warriors coach Steve Kerr, who said the Cavs would've done the same had Love been in the lineup.

"I think the game would've been the same whether he played or not," Kerr said.

POWER LINEUP

Love is averaging 16.5 points and 9.4 rebounds this postseason. His good games have been really good. His bad ones have been really bad.

But again, this may not be about Love so much. It may have more to do with the fact the Cavs only have a maximum of four games to get this right.

And again, the Warriors don't play the game like everyone else. Therefore, they can't be defended like everyone else.

Jefferson may be better equipped to defend the likes of Warriors small forward Harrison Barnes, combo forward Draymond Green, and even shooting guard Klay Thompson.

Jefferson starting at small forward also means LeBron James starting at power forward. That move, more than anything, seemed to pay huge dividends for the Cavs.

In the first two games, Love got switched onto Warriors guard Steph Curry — not something the Cavs are hoping to see. But when the power forward is James, and James gets switched onto Curry — well, that's not always so bad.

Anyway, none of this to say the Cavs will change everything around if Love is able to play Friday. It seems pretty promising that he will.

He very well could start. Or the Cavs could always bring him along slowly, bring him off the bench, and the potential dilemma solves itself.

Either way, Lue may have a decision to make, and with Game 4 being another must-win for the Cavs, it's a pretty important one.

JUNE 13

Cavs angry, aim to save season

Random dribbles on the Cavaliers entering Game 5 of the Finals vs. the Warriors on Monday.

1. This could be the end of the line and the Cavs are indeed approaching it like a Game 7. They trail the Warriors 3-1 and they're on the road.

2. The Cavs had some strong words in discussions with the league office over the weekend. It was centered on what they view to be inconsistent, "selective" officiating.

3. Warriors forward Draymond Green was suspended Sunday for one game. The Cavs only wanted Green to be dealt with according to the rules. They made no major push for a suspension.

4. Instead, the Cavs focused on what is happening near the rim. Their biggest issue is what they view as uncalled fouls when LeBron James drives to the basket – citing 11 different instances of Warriors forward Andre Iguodala whacking James across the arms. None drew a whistle.

5. The Cavs are blaming no one but themselves for their current dilemma. They refuse to use officiating as an excuse — but they do seem to believe games have been called in a manner that prohibits them from executing the game plan. A big part of that game plan entails taking the Warriors to the hole and forcing them to protect the rim without fouling.

6. Nor do the Cavs have a problem with physical basketball. They've initiated some and hope to partake in more. They just seem to feel as if they're getting mugged in the lane, while too many touch fouls have been called at the other end. That was the heart of their message to the league.

7. One member of the Cavs' roster relayed to Amico Hoops: "Bron and

(Kyrie Irving) are getting physically killed in this series. ... We'll see how it goes Monday when the favor is returned."

8. Meanwhile, as suspected, the Warriors reacted angrily to the news of Green's suspension. It resulted in some criticism of James from Warriors guard Klay Thompson. "Guess his feelings just got hurt," Thompson said.

9. One member of the Cavs told Amico Hoops: "We'll be physical and go at them, just as they have. If it turns into something more than that, it will start with them, and we're ready for it. We expect that arena to be hostile, it's a loud place. But (the Warriors) may have just said a little more than they should have."

10. Read: Game 5 should be one heated contest.

JUNE 14

Star power may be Cavs' solution

Random dribbles on the Cavaliers' huge 112-97 win over the host Warriors in Game 5 of the Finals on Monday.

1. This may have been the greatest win in Cavs history and the greatest two-man show in the history of the Finals. I just can't decide who was better — LeBron James, or Kyrie Irving.

2. James finished with 41 points. Irving finished with 41 points. James finished with 16 rebounds – sixteen! He also passed for seven assists. Irving had six assists and was a sizzling 17-of-24 from the floor.

3. This was a remarkably clutch performance by two of the game's brightest stars in a building where so few people have success. Entering Monday, the Warriors were 50-3 at home.

4. Yes, it can be annoying to watch James and Irving go one-on-one or play "iso" basketball from time to time. But when it works, man, it's a thing of beauty. And the Cavs had to have it, as no one else could get anything going.

5. Besides, all LeBron needed last season was one more guy to help. Now, he has it in Irving.

6. So maybe coach Ty Lue and the Cavs are on to something here. That being, to get the ball to LeBron and Kyrie and get out of the way. At least, keep doing it until the Warriors stop it.

7. Seriously. That right there may be the Cavs' best chance to become the first team ever to overcome a 3-1 deficit in the Finals.

8. Either way, the Cavs now have some serious momentum and are returning home. Game 6 is Thursday at The Q. I'll be honest, I had my doubts about typing that.

9. Then again, I predicted in my latest podcast that the Cavs would come back and win the title. I'll stick with it.

10. But J.R. Smith (10 points) cautioned: "Nothing changes. Our backs are against the wall, we gotta come out swinging."

11. The Cavs only passed for 15 assists. They only attempted 24 3-pointers, a lower number for them. They were going to the basket and daring the Warriors to stop them. And man, neither James nor Irving ever got stopped.

12. LeBron's first two baskets of the night were threes. Do you realize how huge that was when you consider his issues from the perimeter the past, oh, two years? He seemed out to prove something, and that something being he can still shoot a little.

13. On the other hand, the Warriors missed 17 of their final 19 threes. Some of that was chance. But some of it was the result of the Cavs making the Warriors fight for every inch just to get a decent look. The Cavs had great energy on defense in the second half.

14. Draymond Green didn't play as he served a one-game suspension. No doubt, it was a factor. The Warriors often go as Green goes. But they still played well enough for three quarters to win. The Cavs just had bigger stars at the end.

15. Kevin Love again played poorly on the road. He did the same in the East finals vs. the Raptors. I don't get it. The guy is better than this. And the Cavs need him more than ever. How he responds will likely determine his future in Cleveland.

16. Meanwhile, Tristan Thompson gave an underrated showing by

collecting 15 boards and creating general havoc for the Warriors.

17. Final thought from LeBron: "We're just happy we got another day. That's all we can ask for. We got another day to survive. We're going to start preparing tonight, start preparing tomorrow, and whenever Game 6 is we'll be ready."

JUNE 15

Can Kyrie, Cavs do it again?

Some random dribbles as we wait for the Cavaliers to face the Warriors in Game 6 of the Finals.

1. Well, no matter the outcome, this is the Cavs' final home game of the season. What happens next will play a major role in how the rest of their summer goes.

2. Two more wins. The Cavs and their fans keep repeating that over and over. Somehow, the Cavs need to beat the Warriors twice — and not lose once. Sounds daunting when you say it out loud.

3. It's a lot of pressure, sure. But I can tell you this: The Cavs are approaching it with the carefree attitude of an underdog. No one expects them to pull this off. They know it will be the Warriors who will be considered the major bust if they fail to win it all.

4. The Warriors were extremely arrogant entering Game 5 at home. Klay Thompson, normally one of the more subdued members of the team, suggested LeBron James needed to man up. Also, Klay's dad, former NBA big man Mychal Thompson, ripped James on his radio show.

5. LeBron responded with 41 points, 16 rebounds and seven assists in an otherworldly Game 5 performance. As one member of the team told me: "It felt good to shut them up. All that matters now is we play with the same fire."

6. Of course, not enough has been said about Kyrie Irving. If he has it figured out as much as it appeared in Game 5, the Warriors could be in trouble. Kyrie gave his best performance of the season when the Cavs needed it most. Can he do it twice more?

7. By the way, Kyrie scored 41 points on 17-of-24 shooting. That made him the first player to shoot 70 percent or better in a 40-point Finals game since the Lakers' Wilt Chamberlain did it in Game 6 of the 1970 Finals vs. the Knicks. Wilt, and now Kyrie.

8. The Cavs are looking to become the first team since the 1966 Lakers (and just the third of 32) to tie a series at 3-all after trailing 3-1.

JUNE 17

Game 7: With LeBron, all is possible

Random dribbles on the Cavaliers' enormous 115-101 win over the Warriors in Game 6 of the Finals on Thursday.

1. Game 7. Did you really think it was possible? Do you even remember that the Cavs were down 3-1? Did you think LeBron James could still carry a team like he has for most of the past two games? I sure didn't.

2. Don't get me wrong. I never doubted James' greatness. I just didn't think he was that guy anymore. I figured he could point the younger Cavs in the right direction. I figured he could show Kyrie Irving, Kevin Love, Tristan Thompson and others what it takes to win a title. But I didn't think he could take over, in the biggest series of the season, all by himself. Not anymore.

3. But LeBron proved me wrong. He's proved a lot of people wrong. He's scored 41 points in back-to-back elimination games. He has his hometown team on the brink of a championship. He has the mighty Warriors feeling nervous.

4. So now, the Cavs are entering the biggest single game in franchise history — and they have LeBron James. And the other guys do not. That has to count for something. It has to count for a lot.

5. LeBron doesn't seem to care that the game is in Oakland. "Doesn't matter to me," he said. "It's Game 7. I'll play anywhere."

6. James later added, "I'm just very chill right now."

7. Irving (23 points) and Thompson (15 points, 16 rebounds) were at James' side as he spoke. Surely, his confidence can be contagious. Kyrie

told the crowd that Game 7 "will be the hardest thing we've ever done in our lives." LeBron says he's chill. Both are taking the right approach.

8. James had a hand in 27 straight points in the second half Thursday, killing the Warriors every time they figured things might go their way. It's a big burden, trying to beat such a young, brash and yes, extremely talented bunch. But the Cavs think they can do it. And James is giving them reason to believe.

9. The odds are against the Cavs. A road team hasn't won Game 7 of the Finals since 1978. That's when the Washington Bullets did it to the Seattle SuperSonics. As my good friend Jeff Phelps of FOX Sports Ohio said, "One of those teams has a different nickname now and the other plays in a different city." Read: It was a long, long time ago.

10. Plus, the Warriors were practically unbeatable at home — and the Cavs already beat them there once. But James is in their heads, on their minds, maybe haunting their dreams. He has a reputation to defend, and he's been on a mission.

11. Yes, he's received some help, particularly from Irving. Thompson and his energy have also been fantastic. J.R. Smith (14 points) hit some important shots, too. And LeBron and Kyrie are gonna need at least one other guy Sunday night. At least one, maybe two.

12. Unfortunately for the Cavs, Love has continued to be way out of sorts. It seems unlikely he'll suddenly pull it together on the biggest night of the year. He just doesn't match up with the Warriors, and at times, it's hurting the Cavs. But if he could just come to life …

13. Either way, nobody really expected the Cavs to get to this point, certainly not after they trailed the series 3-1. Now, they're right back in it. "We've got nothing to lose," Cavs forward Richard Jefferson told FOX Sports Ohio. "All the pressure is on them."

14. Jefferson brings up a valid point — as the Warriors are the defending champs and were heavy favorites entering the playoffs. Even Klay Thompson said they'll be a massive disappointment if they fail to win the title after finishing 73-9.

15. I'm not sure I totally agree with that, and I'm certainly not here to rip anyone. All I know is the Cavs have some momentum, they have LeBron James, and they have the Warriors at least a little on their heels. If you're

the Cavs, that's all a big plus as you take your shot at history.

Game 7: Won't be easy, but Cavs can win

Random dribbles on the Cavaliers, the Warriors and Game 7 of the NBA Finals.

1. Three short summers ago, I was writing about what the Cavaliers should do with the No. 1 overall draft pick. They chose Anthony Bennett.

2. Bennett is no longer in the league. Man, things sure have changed around these parts. Man, the Cavs sure have come a long way.

3. Now, the entire city seems to be in a state of panic. LeBron James returned, and the Cavs are suddenly here — in the first finals Game 7 in franchise history. But I say just enjoy it. Don't get too freaked out. It's basketball. It's fun. It's LeBron and friends. At least it's not Bennett. At least it's not bad.

4. I know the odds are incredibly stacked against the Cavs. I'm not about to argue with those odds. Teams that have trailed a Finals series by a 3-1 deficit are 0-32.

5. Or consider this: The Warriors have never lost three straight under Coach Steve Kerr. Granted, he just took over before the start of last season. Granted, records are there to fall. Granted, I've never seen this Warriors team look more uncertain.

6. If the Cavs do what they did in each of the past two games, I don't care about 0-32, the Warriors' greatness, or a 52-year championship drought. If the Cavs do what they did in each of the past two, they will win the title.

7. Period. No questions asked. Thanks for playing.

8. So what did the Cavs do in the past two? Well, they received an MVP-style performances from James. As good as he was in last season's Finals, he's been even better this year.

9. They also received one 41-point game (Game 5), followed by a fabulous start (Game 6) from Kyrie Irving.

10. So the Cavs rode their stars in the previous two. They mostly rode James, who seems to be more on a mission than ever. He clearly wants to show up Warriors guard and unanimous MVP Steph Curry — and James wants to do it something fierce. He wants to bring a title to Cleveland. He wants his crown as the true king of the NBA. He's willing to do it himself if he has to. He can, and he just might.

11. I think the Warriors miss Andrew Bogut more than they want to admit. Bogut injured his knee in Game 5. And I think Andre Iguodala and Curry are less than 100 percent. I think those things could make the Warriors a very vulnerable team — a team far removed from the one that cruised to 73 wins.

12. I also know Curry, Klay Thompson, Draymond Green and the Warriors are capable of coming to life and burying the opposition via deft passing, strong defense and otherworldly outside shooting.

13. So who will win? I have no idea. I do believe if the Cavs can take care of the ball and score the ball, they'll return home as champs. The Warriors hate it when the Cavs slow them down and keep them out of the transition game. The Cavs have gotten good at that.

14. Will the Cavs do those things? Will Kevin Love, J.R. Smith, Tristan Thompson or maybe someone else suddenly spring to life? Again, I have no clue. But if James and Irving are clicking, well, the Cavs may not need anyone else.

15. Finally, Cavs coach Tyronn Lue has done a nice job getting his team ready, getting his team to believe. He and the Cavs have baffled these Warriors — something I thought I'd never see. And if the Cavs win Sunday, Lue and James and everyone else will likely be bronzed. And rightfully so.

JUNE 20

BELIEVE IT: CAVS, CLEVELAND CHAMPS

I know. It's unreal. It's still hard to believe. But the Cavs are champions. They came back from a 3-1 deficit in the Finals. No team had ever done that. No team had ever defeated Steve Kerr's Warriors three straight. No team … oh, well, you've heard it all by now.

The Cavs just wore down the Warriors. LeBron James, Kyrie Irving and, yes, Kevin Love, Tristan Thompson and J.R. Smith each did something huge at one point in the biggest game of their lives.

The game plan was to let anyone but Steph Curry or Klay Thompson win the game. It resulted in a huge first half for Draymond Green — but just a 12-of-36 shooting night for Curry and Thompson.

In the final 12 minutes, the Cavs took the Warriors out of their rhythm. The Warriors are a rhythm team. But they unraveled. LeBron and the Cavs kept getting stronger.

LeBron told FOX Sports Ohio that his late-game block on Andre Iguodala was "a career-defining moment." James paused, then added, "To do that at that moment."

James finished with 27 points, 11 rebounds, 11 assists. It was the first triple-double in Game 7 of the Finals since James Worthy of the Lakers did it in 1988. Kyrie went for 26 points, including a monster 3-pointer. Smith scored 12, and Love scored nine to go with his 14 rebounds.

Seriously, though. The Cavs now have their own version of The Shot. Kyrie, right over the two-time league MVP. Put the Cavs up three. LeBron hits a free throw later to seal it. Wow.

Kyrie: "I didn't have time to be anything other than myself."

The Cavs are expected to arrive at 11:30 a.m. at the IX Center on Monday.

JUNE 20

The Cavs are champs, and now, so are you

Random dribbles on the Cavaliers' 93-89 championship-clinching win over the host Warriors in Game 7 of the Finals on Sunday.

1. The Warriors went up 3-1 and teased the lion. Big mistake.

2. After the Cavs played mostly soft in their first four games, they called the league office, blasted the refs and promised to get tough. But what actually made them a championship team was they finally decided to play basketball and ride their stars.

3. Cleveland. Champions. I just can't stop saying it, man.

4. I was born in Akron, Ohio. I grew up rooting for the Cavaliers, Indians and Browns. I cover the Cavs for a living. Cleveland sports fans make all of it possible. I'll always be thankful I'm from this area. No fan base is more patient, or more passionate. I couldn't be happier for Northeast Ohio.

5. Yes, I'm rambling. Yes, I'm having trouble sticking with a theme here. I can't really promise this will make sense. It may be in English, but I'm not really sure.

6. So much is still so amazing. So please cut me a little slack. Not that I really need to ask. You're always nice and you always do.

7. The lion referred to earlier is LeBron James, of course. He led the Cavs to two wins on the Warriors' home floor. This after the Warriors barely lost there all season. James responded to lots of criticism by playing what I think was the best basketball of his career. He finished the season with a triple-double: 27 points, 11 rebounds, 11 assists.

8. It was most definitely his best three-game stretch — as James showed Steph Curry something about being the real MVP. James isn't the amazing jump shooter Curry is. But James is the most dominant and most complete player in the game, and it's not even close. Sorry, but Curry doesn't compare.

9. I hate that it's taken me this long to mention Kyrie Irving (26 points). But he played like a champion, and after a season of mostly struggling, Kyrie was at his best when it mattered most. He also hit the biggest shot of

the year, with the game tied, with about a minute remaining. Kyrie rose over Curry and buried the 3-pointer.

10. The Warriors had a few more chances, but you could just tell they stopped believing. Curry, Klay Thompson, Draymond Green – all were stifled by a suffocating Cavs defense at the end.

11. Of course, if you're talking defense, you have to talk about LeBron's monster chase-down block on Andre Iguodala. It saved the day. It changed the momentum. It was just another example that James is truly still king of the NBA.

12. LeBron to FOX Sports Ohio on that very play: "It was a defining moment of my career. To do that in that moment, man …"

13. Kevin Love finished with nine points and 14 huge rebounds. Tristan Thompson had nine points and went 3-of-4 on free throws.

14. But way bigger than what those two did on offense was how they defended. Both did an excellent job of switching out on Warriors shooters Curry and Klay Thompson and creating some havoc on the perimeter.

15. Curry finished with 17 points and went 4-of-14 on threes. Thompson had 14 on 2-of-10 shooting on threes. Definitely pedestrian numbers from the league's best backcourt during the regular season.

16. Kyrie had his way with Curry during their last stint with USA Basketball, and I felt Irving outplayed Curry again here. If LeBron hadn't won MVP, it should've gone to Kyrie.

17. Richard Jefferson told FOX Sports Ohio that he will now retire. He was such a huge part of this. The Cavs will be sad to see him go.

18. I do suspect the Cavs will make some minor changes. I doubt anything sweeping is on the way. I suspect Love will stay. LeBron will be a free agent again, but he's not going anywhere. The Cavs will also have to figure out how to re-sign J.R. Smith, who was huge with his second-half shooting in Game 7.

19. For the most part, Tyronn Lue was outstanding. He won a championship in half a season as head coach. Can't imagine that's ever been done.

20. Cavs GM David Griffin also deserves tons of credit for refusing to let anything derail the Cavs' championship dreams. He changed coaches at midseason — a risky and maybe even unpopular move. But Lue was the best man for the job, and there's no doubting that now. Griffin has molded a roster that fits around LeBron.

21. I'll have plenty more to say in the coming weeks. For now, just enjoy this, Cavs fans. And say it out loud, because Cleveland really is a champion. The drought is over. And I know it feels fantastic.

22. Finally, LeBron: "I'm coming home with what I said I was going to do. I can't wait to get off that plane, hold that trophy up and see all our fans at the terminal."

BONUS DRIBBLES

JULY 8

Are Cavs and Dunleavy a match?

Mike Dunleavy is headed to the Cavaliers following a trade with the Bulls.

How might Dunleavy fit? Let's take a look:

PROS

1. Dunleavy is 6-foot-9 and capable of filling three roles: Shooting guard, small forward, and even power forward as a "stretch four" when Cavs coach Tyronn Lue goes small.

2. Dunleavy was drafted with the No. 3 overall pick (by the Warriors) in 2002. He is a career 44 percent shooter and 80 percent on free throws. The Cavs will be his fifth team. He's seen it all.

3. His specialty is the long-range shot, as Dunleavy hit nearly 40 percent of his 3-pointers during an injury-plagued 2015-16.

4. Even at the advanced NBA age of 35, he is still fairly athletic and will bring a serious, tough and professional approach to the locker room and bench.

5. Cavs general David Griffin didn't need to trade an actual body to obtain Dunleavy. Instead, Griffin is using some salary-cap space — obtained via the Matthew Dellavedova deal to the Bucks.

6. Landing Dunleavy was part of the Bulls' decision to sign Dwyane Wade. And the Cavs still have the entire trade exception ($9.7 million) from the Anderson Varejao deal with Portland. Read: For the Cavs, Dunleavy comes at the right price.

CONS

1. Back surgery limited Dunleavy to 31 games last season, the second-lowest total of his career. He also averaged 7.2 points, the fewest since his rookie season way back in 2002-03.

2. He will be 36 years old when the season starts. Questions exist about his overall durability.

3. Dunleavy isn't likely to do much beyond spot-up shoot. He averaged just 2.7 rebounds and 1.3 assists for the Bulls last season. Some of that may have been due to the injury. We're probably about to find out.

Overall, Dunleavy was a steal of a deal, someone who "LeBron James has long coveted as teammate," according to ESPN.

Dunleavy was also said to be excited about his trade to the defending champions — and if he can stay healthy, he gives the Cavs the type of veteran shooter in reserve every team covets.

Give the Cavs an "A" on this one.

JULY 9

Cavs take Vegas, aim for summer surprise

They will be coached by real NBA coaches and wear jerseys that say "Cleveland" on the front.

They might catch a glimpse of a basketball star in the stands or have a conversation with a big-time scout.

For the 13 members of the Cavaliers' summer roster competing in Las Vegas this week, it truly will be a time for dreams. They'll be pro basketball players for no less than seven days.

But for some, it will be the last time anyone calls them NBA players.

So what are the Cavs hoping to find?

"NBA talent," said assistant GM Trent Redden, the man who sets the Cavs' summer vision. "It sounds simple, but that's really all it is."

On the bright side, the Cavs are confident at least a few such summer players exist.

Shooting guard Jordan McRae will be there, and he finished the season on the regular roster and picked up a championship ring along the way.

Rookie point guard Kay Felder will be there, too — and the Cavs thought highly enough of Felder to buy a second-round pick just to draft him.

But mostly, summer league is one massive search for guys "who may have slipped through the cracks, for whatever reason," Redden said.

It could be because the player wasn't a good fit somewhere else. It could be because the player is a late-bloomer. It could be because he simply didn't get a long enough look by another team.

None of it matters now. Not this week. The Cavs want help. And they want someone to show he really belongs. They want NBA talent.

"If you can find a guy that makes your roster, you're ahead of the game," Redden said.

That may not be so easy for the Cavs, who won the first championship in franchise history less than a month ago. They did it with a star-laden bunch, a group that includes the likes of LeBron James, Kyrie Irving,

Tristan Thompson and Kevin Love.

The bench is even older — with veterans such as Richard Jefferson (35) and Channing Frye (33) playing major roles. Mike Dunleavy was just added via trade and he'll turn 36 before the season. So will James Jones. And Mo Williams is 33.

YOUTH CAN BE SERVED

But the fact the Cavs have so many 30-somethings may actually be a good thing for summer hopefuls.

The Cavs aren't desperate for youth, but it's always nice to have around.

"On top of that, we lack draft picks," Redden said. "So we need to use other ways to find a young guy who fits and can grow with the roster."

Redden, director of pro player personnel Koby Altman, director of D-League operations Mike Gansey and Cavs GM David Griffin never really stop looking for that type of talent — and assembling the summer roster can sometimes be a mad scramble that starts as early as January.

"You try to get guys early, but even then, some will leave for what they see as a better opportunity," Redden explained.

As for the ones who are here now, McRae and Felder are perhaps the most well-known. But the Cavs, of course, will thoroughly evaluate all.

Swingman DeAndre Liggins, point guard Michael Stockton, and forwards Raphiael Putney and Kenny Gabriel — who Redden compared to a young James Jones and described as "a big wing shooter" — are just some of the others to watch.

"We want to find guys who fit the culture and maybe have that one NBA skill where they can possibly flourish," Redden said.

For one week, the 13 members of the Cavs' summer roster get the chance to prove they can be that guy.

Mostly, they are hoping what happens in Vegas doesn't stay in Vegas. They want to be pro basketball players in training camp, too.

JULY 26

Lue fits, and Cavs proving they know it

For the Cavaliers and their coach, there was never a moment of doubt.

Tyronn Lue won a championship. General manager David Griffin and the people running the Cavs were sold on Lue even before that.

So it only made sense for the Cavs to offer Lue a contract extension — and for Lue to accept. The players respect him, he never stopped believing in them, and he was the man in charge when Cleveland broke its 52-year title drought.

An agreement on the extension was reportedly reached Monday. It's for five years and worth $35 million, according to league sources.

Yahoo Sports was the first to report the news of Lue and the Cavs.

And what's not to like about Lue?

He was charged with what seemed like an impossible task. He was expected to improve a 30-11 team.

That was the Cavs' record when David Blatt was fired at midseason. Remember, Blatt took an injury-plagued team to the NBA Finals last year.

Then Lue took over, and the Cavs went 27-14 in this season's second half. That was three wins less than Blatt compiled in the first half.

Blatt and the Cavs lost to the Warriors in six games, but Lue pushed the Cavs back to the finals. They trailed the Warriors 3-1 with Game 5 on the Warriors' home court.

It was over.

Or was it?

None of the previous 32 teams that trailed a finals series 3-1 had come back to win. Lue and the Cavs improved that record to 1-32.

Yes, LeBron James, Kyrie Irving and the men in uniform had a lot to do with that. But Lue did, too.

His style wasn't to scream Bobby Knight-like proclamations throughout the gym. He didn't give his players serious Gregg Popovich-like stares.

Lue led by keeping his composure, never getting too high or low. He was even-keel, and even when all seemed lost, so was his team.

This isn't to crown Lue as the second coming of Red Auerbach or Phil Jackson, or even the forever-underrated Doc Rivers. Lue may be there someday.

Right now, he's just the best coach for James, Irving, Kevin Love and the rest of this particular bunch. And the Cavs apparently believe he will be that coach for quite some time.

It's hard to blame them.

Lue shaped the Cavs into a champion. It was only a matter of time before they opened their pocketbooks to prove he's their man.

AUGUST 22

Kyrie Irving, Champion. Again.

When the Cavaliers drafted Kyrie Irving in 2011, I didn't exactly map out plans to cover the NBA Finals.

Irving seemed like a nice point guard, a kid who could handle the ball with a good outside shot, but a little questionable on defense.

He did look like the best player in that particular draft, though, and then-general manager Chris Grant made the right choice with the No. 1 overall pick.

So everyone considered Irving a fine player — but not many seemed to consider him a big winner.

It may be time to rethink that.

Irving struck gold as a member of the U.S. Olympic basketball team Sunday, when the Americans downed Serbia 96-66 in Rio de Janeiro.

This after Irving won a championship with the Cavaliers in June.

In the finals, Irving made the biggest 3-pointer of the season, then created the biggest almost-assist when he passed to LeBron James for a monster almost-dunk.

Irving's three gave the Cavs a three-point lead. James was fouled on the dunk attempt, and his free throw extended it to four with 10.6 seconds left.

Game, set, first title in franchise history.

And Irving truly was Mr. Fourth Quarter, outplaying Warriors guard and two-time MVP Steph Curry on his own home floor in the season's most meaningful moments.

It was Irving who hit the final basket, it was Irving who controlled the game, it was Curry who failed to get around the Cavs' swarm of taller defenders.

Some people wouldn't have believed it possible back in 2011.

Irving barely played his lone college season at Duke, a toe injury keeping him on the bench.

He gained a reputation earlier in his career as being injury-prone. Last season, he was coming off knee surgery and his game looked clunky at the start. But if there's one thing we're learning about Irving, it's that he knows how to finish at winning time.

All this and he's still just 24 years old.

WINNING WAYS

It's true that his real success didn't come until James returned to the Cavs, until Kevin Love arrived in a trade, until Tristan Thompson (drafted fourth in 2011) morphed into an energy big man.

GM David Griffin also played a major role by bringing in older locker-room voices.

So for Irving, it didn't happen until a team was built around him. But guess what? Welcome to the NBA. No one does it alone — at least not when the idea is winning championships.

With Team USA, Irving got to play alongside the likes of Kevin Durant, Paul George and Carmelo Anthony. All are accomplished pros.

Still, just like the Cavs, it's clear the Americans needed Irving.

He's not a throwback point guard, holding up his fist, calling out plays and patiently making sure everyone is in their proper place.

Irving is much more likely to drive and score in traffic with dazzling moves at the hoop — or drive and kick if the first option doesn't work.

That's not to say he's selfish. Just the opposite. He knows how to play next to other stars. Mostly, he's just good.

How's that for expert analysis?

But when it comes to Irving, there's really no other way to spin it. Some guys just got it, and he's one.

Only James, Michael Jordan and Scottie Pippen had won a gold medal and an NBA championship in the same year. Irving is on that list now, too.

It's a pretty good list. It's a list full of big-time winners.

Irving belongs there now, and here's the thing: He may be just getting started.

ABOUT THE AUTHOR

Sam Amico has written about the NBA for more than 15 years for various newspapers, magazines and websites. A writer and broadcaster for FOX Sports Ohio, his coverage of pro basketball has appeared in *USA Today*, the *Boston Herald* and the *New York Post*. He is the author of *A Basketball Summer* and the founding editor of AmicoHoops.net. He lives in Medina, Ohio, with his wife Katie and their three children.

For more coverage of the Cavaliers and NBA from Sam Amico, visit:

AmicoHoops.net

55691729R00111

Made in the USA
Lexington, KY
01 October 2016